DUBLIN : A PORTRAIT

DUBLIN

A PORTRAIT

by V. S. Pritchett

PHOTOGRAPHS BY

Evelyn Hofer

THE BODLEY HEAD

LONDON SYDNEY
TORONTO

The author and the publishers wish to thank the following for permission to quote material from the publications listed: Hutchinson & Co Ltd: *Short History of Ireland* by J. C. Beckett; Routledge & Kegan Paul Ltd: *Round the Black Church* by Austin Clarke; David Higham Associates Ltd: *Dublin 1660–1810* by Maurice Craig; Methuen & Co Ltd: *Kevin O'Higgins* by Terence de Vere White; Jonathan Cape Ltd and The Viking Press Inc: *A Portrait of the Artist as a Young Man* by James Joyce; The Society of Authors: *Finnegan's Wake* by James Joyce; Patrick Kavanagh: his *Collected Poems*; Macmillan & Co Ltd, The Macmillan Company of Canada Ltd and Crowell-Collier & Macmillan Inc: *Inishfallen Fare Thee Well* by Sean O'Casey; Macmillan & Co Ltd, The Macmillan Company of Canada and St Martin's Press Inc: *The Plough and the Stars* by Sean O'Casey; Rupert Hart-Davis Ltd and Atlantic-Little, Brown & Company: *I Remember! I Remember!* by Sean O'Faolain; The Society of Authors: *John Bull's Other Island* by G. Bernard Shaw; Methuen & Co Ltd: '*The Body's Imperfection*' by L. A. G. Strong; Christy & Moore Ltd: *The Face and Mind of Ireland* by Aarland Ussher; A. P. Watt & Son and Crowell-Collier & Macmillan Inc: '*Remorse for Intemperate Speech*' by W. B. Yeats.

Printed and bound in Switzerland for
THE BODLEY HEAD LTD
9 Bow Street, London W C 2
by Conzett & Huber, Zurich
First published 1967

bailiú eile
(NEXT COLLECTION)

3.0 P.M

bosca (BOX)
uaire bailite
(HOURS of COLLECTION)

laete seactaine
(WEEKDAYS)

4. P.M

11. A.M

8. P.M EX. SAT.

Dé Domnaig 3. P.M
(SUNDAY)

Ní ceart leitreaca le hairgead etc.
do cur sa bosca so, act ba ceart
iad a cláru.

(LETTERS CONTAINING COIN ETC, SHOULD NOT BE
POSTED IN THIS BOX BUT SHOULD BE REGISTERED)

I

Dublin as it is; Dublin as it was. I must declare my interest. It is very personal. If I were to write an account of my education the city of Dublin would have to appear as one of my schoolmasters, a shabby, taunting, careless, half-laughing reactionary. His subject? History, of course. I did in fact have such an Irish master at my London school. His name was Callaghan; he glittered with mocking amusement during school prayers and was famous for his tempers, his personal disasters and his scorn. After reading something I had written, he delighted himself and our class by demonstrating to all of us, and with exact command of language, that I was raving mad. When I first came to Dublin, he was often in my mind.

This was in January 1923 when I crossed the Irish Channel as a very young journalist to write about the Civil War. I spent two separate years there, with a long interval between in Spain. I had been living in Paris and arrived in Dublin innocently wearing a broad-brimmed green velour hat and a trench coat: if you add a revolver, I was the very picture—only less dismal—of that gunman whose statue adds nothing to the aesthetic attractions of Athlone. My equipment was quickly stolen from me by protective friends. At Westland Row I stepped out into the sleet, and into the smell of horse manure that was the general smell of Dublin in those days and drove by outside car to an hotel in Harcourt Street. It was, to my astonishment, a temperance hotel. The jarvey, who was drunkish, whipped up his fast little pony and delivered a long speech full of Bedads, Begobs, and Please Gods and with asides about the terrible state of 'the unfortunate country' as we drove; he turned out to be a Cockney. Dubliners and Cockneys have a cheerful taste for disguise, and a common adenoidal quality in their vowels.

The worst of the Civil War was over in Dublin but one was frequently stopped by military patrols in the street and searched for arms; there were raids by lorry loads of troops in the night. There were occasional rifle shots. One explosion brought the soot down the chimney of my room—and comments from the chambermaid. But the war had moved to the south-west and after a while

Past and Present

3

I followed it there, spending my evenings with commercial travellers who paid no attention to the Troubles, in going to hear an English Shakespeare company who were playing to packed houses in Cork and other places. The line in Hamlet saying that everyone in England was mad—thereby confirming my schoolmaster—was wildly cheered.

My first Irish friends were boundlessly hospitable, of course, but they pointed out to me that I belonged to a fleshly, materialist, sensual nation given to sex, the love of money and over-eating. This could have been true for I have met the same remark in Aarland Ussher's *The Face and Mind of Ireland;* but I must point out that Dublin was then, and still is, a city where very fat, black-haired, red-faced men abound, men as soft and plump as tenors in training. This is said to be due to a diet of Guinness and Dublin's excellent bread. For myself, in two years of Ireland, I faded away to wanness in that languid climate and was rarely able to get up before eleven in the morning. I became sensitive, snobbish and fey: this was much noticed when eventually I returned to England. I was even to come across a Quaker ex-Auxiliary who had settled down with an Irish Catholic girl in Tipperary—a county he had probably terrorised a couple of years before—who had the same characteristics. Something odd happens to the English in Ireland. And to the Irish in England: my schoolmaster, who was an Irish Catholic, denied he was either Irish or Catholic when we attacked him about his politics.

My knowledge of history was small—in any case I am inclined to believe poets and imaginative writers rather than historians—but what there was, I soon discovered, was disadvantageous. My family were firm *Manchester Guardian* liberals and Home Rulers. That condemned me from the start. My grandfather thought Gladstone was God and some historians have malignly suggested he probably was. Such views appealed to no one in a country which is innately illiberal where, as in Scotland, there is more feeling for the Devil than for the Almighty. My next disadvantage was that as a child in 1912 I had taken part in a small suburban concert in our part of London, a concert run by local Fabians, in order to collect money on behalf of Jim Larkin's dock strike, the strike that brought James Connolly's labour movement into the Easter Rising; this involuntary precocity on my part was more sensible than I could know. I had also listened to Percy French's anecdotes and songs at school; and in 1923 Percy French was 'out', just as Somerville and Ross were. (I was delighted to hear this year in Dublin that they are 'in' again; the imaginary, synthetic Gaelic Irishman appears to be fading.) Finally, an Irish

Right
A Dublin sky

Next two pages
College Green

stationer in Streatham gave me a copy of McCabe's *Priests and People in Ireland*, warmly urging me to conceal it and never to get into a religious or political argument. My only useful equipment was a heavy suitcase full of books by Yeats, AE, Synge, Lady Gregory, James Stephens and others. These were moderately approved of by the startled Free State soldiers who once or twice came barging into my room on some raid or other at three in the morning. One, I recall, stopped to read a poem.

They were nasty times, often comical, often horrible. Dublin had had a terrible six years since the Rising: the 'war' was degenerating into gangsterism. The politicals were suffering from strain and many were out of their minds. The public was, quite rightly, weary of the business, just as in Europe people were sick of the 1914 war and its aftermath. Harsh and obstructive as the British had been, the liberated Irish were colder and harsher to one another, as Lord Birkenhead had predicted they would be. There was jealousy among the leaders. The scale though not the savagery of the Troubles was greatly exaggerated; every week houses were burned down—thirty-seven country houses, some of them very fine—or robbed, and people were murdered or killed in action, the word varying with your politics. There was continual talk of 'principle' but, in fact, personal jealousy and vengeance were at the bottom of these actions which have left a deep bitterness that lasts among the survivors of my generation and my few elders to this day. In Dublin nowadays, if you ask about this crime or that, the memory has to be avoided; it is invariably described as 'a mistake'.

O'Connell Street was still largely in ruins. It had been one of the finest streets in Europe; and on the rubble, some of the fanatical women fighters of the time would scream at their tiny audiences. There were processions—and Dublin is a processional city—appealing for the release of the political prisoners. Among them Frank O'Connor, later a dear friend of mine, and I regret to say that at that time I could not have sympathised with him. There would be occasional days when in St Stephen's Green you would notice two's and threes of men, armed with heavy sticks, gradually moving across the city until by the time they got to O'Connell Bridge they turned into threatening hundreds. The government buildings were surrounded by sand bags and barbed wire. In the Dail the new government, led by the clever and dogged little Cosgrave, was young and astonished people by its political aptitude. Cosgrave stood out because of his experience of government, his quick humour and his courage. He was the perfect exemplar, in that

Halloween

5

period, of the ordinary man suddenly elevated to high office, who had the inborn moral character that is required for rule. It was a delight to hear this little fighter with the gay brushed-up hair, in debate. I remember O'Higgins's blistering tongue and also his gravity. Astonishing that a man so young should have been so formed and so fit for the demands of revolution and government. Ireland will never give him a statue.

The English had expected a circus; but in fact, in the most serious sense, the Irish had created a Parliament. It was the one hopeful thing in a city torn by private rancour underneath the surface; though outwardly the old Edwardian life still went on. Poor women still wore the black shawl, there were hundreds of barefooted children, the jarveys were drunk more often than not; one heard derelict ballad singers in the streets. You were addressed as 'Your honour' by beggars and 'Whatever you say yourself' seemed to be the answer to every question. The symbol of Dublin's Edwardian ease was that eternal, giant policeman who used to direct the traffic at the bottom of Grafton Street and who had inspired one of James Stephens's novels. A lady jay-walker whom I knew nipped through the traffic one day and stood by him, saying 'I think it will be safer if I stand with you in the middle'. To this the giant replied 'And with me, ma'am, you'll only be middling safe'. That described the sensation one had in Dublin. You picnicked in the Dublin mountains, but you passed the rough wooden cross—as it was then—that marked the place where Lemass, the brother of the present Taoiseach or Prime Minister, was 'killed in action' or 'murdered'. Walking home to my lodgings in Waterloo Road one summer evening, I collided with a young man who came hurrying round the corner and who put a revolver in my stomach. 'Sorry', he said and ran away. It was an instance, I suppose, of Dublin playing up.

For myself, these sights, words and experiences were strange and at first exhilarating, and Dublin captivates, in any case, by the purity and languor of its air and the beauty of its situation. The English, as distinct from the English State, have rarely been disliked in Ireland (the Black and Tans represented the English State); as for the troops, most Irishmen love a soldier even if they kill him. The Scots, the Welsh and the English and the Irish, those cantankerous and mixed races that have been maliciously forced to share these islands and have colonised widely in order to get away from their quarrel, have learned to mock one another. The Irish Troubles were, in an important sense, a continuation of the

The Dail

6

DÁIL ÉIREANN.

PAIDIR.

IARRAIMID Ort, a Thiarna, T'anál naomhtha do chur fúinn chun sinn do stiúradh in ár ngníomhartha agus neart do ghrásta do bhronnadh orainn chun iad do thabhairt chun críche, ionnus gur Uait-se tosnófar ár n-uile bhriathar agus ár n-uile ghníomh feasta, agus gur Tríot a críochnófar iad; tré Chríost ár dTiarna.

PRAYER.

DIRECT, we beseech Thee, O Lord, our actions by Thy holy inspirations and carry them on by Thy gracious assistance; that every word and work of ours may always begin from Thee, and by Thee be happily ended; through Christ Our Lord. Amen.

European revolution caused by the European war: the two parties in Ireland who were uniquely aware of this were the urban workers and the Anglo-Irish, both of which have come poorly out of the struggle and both of which were more European than they were patriots. But a class revolution had taken place and the Anglo-Irish who left in tens of thousands, and who shook their fists at the Dublin mountains as the mail boat took them out of Dunleary, knew this. The strangeness of the Irish situation lay in its contradictions. One was taken back thirty to fifty years into the domestic scenes of a Victorian novel, into unbelievable gentilities and snobberies. People had tea parties. They lived on cake. One was back in Mrs Gaskell's country world; and at the same time was thrown forward into the first conflict of colonialism, as my friend Sean O'Faolain says in his autobiography, a foretaste of events in India, Cyprus and Africa. One was being pushed out of purely Irish history into the modern world of small, young, emancipated states which would have to make their minds up about nationalism and social revolution. Ireland dodged the issue by creating a Catholic middle class; but its present situation does not differ greatly from those of the Eastern European satellites in 1945. 'Ould Ireland' had vanished. Ireland was now young and new and was to become alarmingly on its own and to lose the importance, as a state, to which the great gifts of its scattered people had entitled it. It began its new existence as a gamble; fortunately that is irresistible to Irish people, who move easily from torpor to recklessness.

'You cannot conquer Ireland, you cannot extinguish the Irish passion for freedom', Pearse had said.

The gamble, in this century, began in the Easter Rising in 1916, the tragic, muddled fiasco that was to turn into a triumph because it created heroes and martyrs. It was followed by the guerilla war against the British. The scene in central Dublin at Easter 1916 has been compared to Ypres in the same year, and Dublin had the distinction of being the first capital city in Europe to be wrecked by war in this century. The fact contains a temptation to exaggerate; the losses after the Easter Rising have been put at 1,351 people killed or wounded and about 170 houses destroyed. As I have said, whether Dubliners knew it or not, Dublin was having its share of the European revolution of those years; one man, James Connolly, knew it. He was a social revolutionary. The other leaders of the Rising belonged to the 'physical force' traditions of the Irish struggle; they had seized control of Sinn Fein, whose policy was the pacific wearing away of

Lounge Bar

lazy British rule. Once Ulster, backed by British Tories, had raised their armed Volunteers in the north, the raising and arming of Volunteers in the south was inevitable. And, as before in Irish history, there was the attempt (always a failure) to get in foreign aid. The lesson seems to be the paradoxical one that in Ireland's isolated position, the enemy was more reliable than the so-called allies— he was at any rate *there* to fight and beat.

In an article in the *Daily Telegraph* of Easter Monday, fifty years later, Terence de Vere White makes an important point about the Rising when he says:

> There were two elements in the Rising—poetry and poverty. It is the poetry that, in a desperate and dotty way, has survived.
>
> Had Connolly, as he was prepared and determined to, made his own protest in arms on behalf of the Dublin slum dwellers, the horror of whose conditions had been exposed in 1913, his effort would have been able to show, after the October Revolution in Russia, that Ireland had narrowly escaped Bolshevism. Without Pearse and his friends a Rising would have been smaller, more quickly suppressed and, in the long run, unavailing.

From 1912 onward it was a common sight to see uniformed and armed Volunteers parading and even conducting manoeuvres in the streets. There had more than once been mock attacks on the Post Office which the public took as a regular part of city entertainment, Dublin streets being notably full of life. After the dock strike in 1912 when Connolly formed his 'workers' army', one could see ragged, barefooted children marching up and down with sticks on their shoulders, copying their elders. The British, gripped by the German struggle, were anxious not to provoke the Irish after 1914, and did little or nothing to interfere. If rebellion was in the air, they relied on an extremely efficient espionage and code-breaking system which would enable them to pounce on the leaders if things became dangerous. And Irish rebellions have been notoriously amateur and subject to disunity. The British knew in detail of Casement's venture. But their officials failed to make up their minds quickly enough about the pouncing; and, on the Irish side, there was muddle. The Rising was countermanded; but Pearse and Connolly went through with it, knowing their gesture was suicidal. The number of Volunteers collected on the famous day was small compared with the total number of the movement. This makes their effort all the more remarkable.

The story has often been told. The British troops (a large number of new recruits, for the seasoned soldiers were fighting in France alongside Irish

Glasnevin, a republican's grave

regiments) were scarce on the Easter Morning. As many as could had gone off to the Fairyhouse races; so that in fact the key point of the Castle was left with little more than a corporal's guard. The small band of Volunteers who shot the sentry and tied up the guard had no idea that the place was empty; awed by their achievement they retired to positions in a neighbouring newspaper office and lost an enormous chance. The Post Office was easily occupied. A detachment walked into the vast hall, where a memorial to the Rising now stands, frightened off the clerks and, catching a British officer who had gone in to send a telegram or buy a postal order, locked him up in a telephone box outside. From this he had a ringside view. Then outside the Post Office, Pearse proclaimed the Irish Republic in words that take one back to Wolfe Tone and the ideals of the French Revolution—ideals which have a limited appeal to the Irish public, as later writers often remind us. Even so, the moment was a fine one; no criticism can dim it and it reminds one of how long Dublin remained an 18th-century city. For many hours, half-empty Dublin was dazed by the lazy spring morning; but soon the barricades were going up, British troops were hurriedly brought in and then house-to-house street fighting and artillery bombardment began. At Boland's Mills near Ballsbridge, de Valera held out. He has been reproached for failing to relieve the hard-pressed insurgents who in the 'Battle of Mount Street' kept a whole English battalion pinned down but he cleverly deceived the gunners of the *Helga* who were shelling the city. One could go on with the frightening struggle in the corridors and wards of the Nurses' Home.

Presently O'Connell Street was on fire. Regular troops, especially in those days, were at a great disadvantage in this kind of fighting; a relatively few Volunteers could hold down a company. The fighting became a horrible affair of breaking into houses, moving from corridor to corridor. There were snipers on church towers. At Portobello, an Irish officer serving with the British went mad and started executing prisoners in cold blood. Among those he murdered was Skeffington, James Joyce's pacifist friend, who had gone out to try and stop the fighting and rescue the wounded. The Countess Markievicz, retreating from St Stephen's Green to the College of Surgeons, and with the ferocity of the women who engaged in the struggle then and in the Civil War, asked where the knives were for hand-to-hand fighting. The bodies of men, women and children were lying in streets and gardens. When the insurgents were unable to hold Linenhall Barracks any longer they sloshed drums of oil and paint in one of the rooms and set the place on fire. Terrible things and odd things occurred: when Bridewell Police Station was taken—according to Max Caulfield's excellent narrative—twenty-four policemen were found hiding in the cells.

Since those days the difficulties of street fighting and guerilla warfare in cities have become familiar. It is still astonishing that Pearse's forces held the city for a week against thousands of troops and artillery fire. The mass of Dubliners hated the Rising. They insulted and abused the insurgents; in Moore Street, the market women threw vegetables and chamberpots at them. They blamed Pearse's men for the destruction and deaths and, if there were outcries against atrocities committed by one British regiment, the sympathies were with the British. The awful slums of Dublin poured out their looters. The mob smashed into shops, crowds of children went after the toys, and near Parnell's monument the mob lit a bonfire and danced round it, while the shooting went on, and the ambulances went by. Ten years later Sean O'Casey, who had been in the Irish Citizen's Army and who had lived in the Dublin tenements, got closer than anyone to what Dublin felt. One hears a voice that could be Pearse's:

> Comrade Soldiers of the Irish Volunteers and of the Citizen Army, we rejoice in this terrible war. The old heart of the earth needed to be warmed with the red wine of the battlefields.... Such august homage were never offered to God as this: the homage of millions of lives given gladly for love of country. And we must be ready to pour out the wine in the same glorious sacrifice, for without shedding of blood there is no redemption.

And then we see Bessie Burgess, the old Orange termagant who has been denouncing her Sinn Fein neighbours and upholding the good old Protestant cause, come rushing in in the third act of *The Plough and the Stars*, wearing a new hat, a fox fur, and carrying three umbrellas and a box of biscuits.

> They're breakin' into th' shops, they're breakin' into th' shops! Smashin' th' windows, batterin' in th' doors an' whippin' away everything! An' th' Volunteers is firin' on them. I seen two men an' a lassie pushin' a piano down th' street, an' th' sweat rollin' off them thryin' to get it on th' pavement; an' an oul' wan that must ha' been seventy lookin' as if she'd dhrop every minute with th' dint o' heart beatin', thryin' to pull a big double bed out of a broken shop window! I was goin' to wait till I dhressed meself from th' skin out.

The opportunity is too much for the tenement, but even the joy of plunder does not unite the Catholic and Protestant:

Veteran of the Rising

It's a fat whondher to Jeanie Gogan (cries Mrs Gogan) that a lady-like singer o' hymns like yourself would lower her thoughts from sky thinkin' to sthretch out her arm in a sly seekin' way to pinch anything dhriven ashtray in th' confusion of th' battle our boys is makin' for th' freedom of their counthry.

To which Bessie replies with the real voice of slumdom:

Poverty an' hardship has sent Bessie Burgess to abide with sthrange company, but she always knew them she had to live with from backside to breakfast time: an' she can tell them, always havin' had a Christian kinch on her conscience, that a passion for thievin' an' pinchin' would find her soul a foreign place to live in, an' that her present intention is quite th' lofty-hearted one of pickin' up anything shaken up an' scatthered about in th' loose confusion of a general plundher.

Then it was all over. Hunger and exhaustion defeated the rebels, but the defeat turned into a triumph. The British executed the leaders and sent others to life imprisonment. The gallows and the prison have always been the shrines of Irish freedom. It would be inaccurate to say all southern Ireland was now united, for Sinn Fein had a large number of enemies, but Ireland had woken up from its Victorian sleep.

In the years between 1918 and 1923 Dublin saw the worst kind of warfare—guerilla warfare in terms of assassination and bomb throwing, secret sentences, executions, murders at night. There was a curfew, Auxiliary police and the detestable Black and Tans patrolled the streets. One cannot pass certain houses without remembering Bloody Sunday. One cannot look at the walls of Kilmainham and Mountjoy Prisons or Arbour Hill Barracks, without thinking of the execution squads. By 1921, Dubliners were exhausted and on the point of nervous breakdown; family or sectarian hatreds had reached an intolerable pitch and brutal muddle on the British side began to be matched by hysteria and jealousy among the Sinn Fein leaders. Differences which were metaphysical became violent, because the habit of violence had grown. The Four Courts were occupied and bombarded; in the course of this the Irish suffered a loss which was hardly noticed at the time but the humiliation of which has been lasting: the loss of their archives. As always, revolution consumed its own children. Leader after leader was killed. Many of them felt—what one of them told me—that retribution would fall upon them for their own blood guilt. They did what they felt they had to do; many were broken; but they would have to pay the price. Among the younger people—in 1923—there was a strong feeling that the extreme side

The Four Courts

was the more honourable; extremism and lawlessness having a traditional prestige. Kevin O'Higgins was, I thought, most conscious of the tragic nature of his role, a young man who knew what the burden of a post-revolutionary government was. Whenever I saw him he talked quietly. One saw by his ironical look and his reserved humour that he looked pityingly but kindly at a young reporter like myself, for he lived on another planet. His terrible experience had indeed set him apart. He had to use the firing squad against his own people. It is better to hear an Irishman, Terence de Vere White, speaking of this in his life of O'Higgins:

> The relatively small proportion of the population engaged in the conflict with Great Britain acted in concert up to December 1921. The split which then occurred involved more than a mere political difference. Personal loyalties and, perhaps, jealousies played their part. There were many who took sides against the Treaty who had their spiritual home on the constitutional side and there were those who followed Collins who would have been equally happy on the hillsides. And thousands took arms against the Government who had taken no part against the British. Revolutions throw to the surface fierce and dangerous men as pure-souled idealists. These were men who shot down policemen or British soldiers to order but who were quite incapable of enunciating any political theory. They took to violence as a duck to water and revelled in a revolutionary period. These are the men who are misfits in normal times, who clutch at Nazism, Fascism, Mosleyism and, in Ireland, at the I.R.A. as an outlet for their anti-social impulses.

And the I.R.A. itself had two factions. Its fortunes have gone up and down in the last forty years of Irish government, but supported by American money it still manages the occasional raid, murder or explosion. Many of its members blow themselves up with their home-made bombs. Others die after lonely misery abroad. It is forbidden to print the letters I.R.A. in the Press; Dublin, always in love with euphemism, darkly knows it 'as an illegal organisation'. At the moment it is feeble though perhaps the blowing up of Nelson's Pillar in 1966 acted like sympathetic magic on their declining potency.

This book is neither a history of Irish politics nor of Irish literature, but if I turn now to literature it is because for twenty years, prior to 1923, Dublin became famous for the Irish literary revival, and the effort of the Gaelic League to recover the almost extinguished Irish language. This movement, which ran parallel with the rise of Sinn Fein and sometimes mingled with it, can be said to have begun about 1878. The leading names in the literary revival were Anglo-Irish and Protestant: Standish O'Grady, Douglas Hyde (who became the first President of the Irish Republic and whose feeling for the cultural de-anglicisation

Right
Frank O'Connor

Next two pages
Killiney Bay

of Ireland must have appealed to de Valera), Yeats, AE, Lady Gregory, James Stephens, Synge, John Eglinton. The news of a 'new literature' reached George Moore in Paris and he came over to see the beginnings of the Irish theatre. It was immediately in trouble with some of the Catholic bishops and with the British authorities in the Castle before the Rising; it was often in trouble with Sinn Fein. The Revival can be said to be the swan song of the Anglo-Irish and their immortal contribution to the new national consciousness; and although there have been distinguished Irish writers since that time—figures like Sean O'Faolain, Frank O'Connor, Liam O'Flaherty, Patrick Kavanagh, Flann O'Brien and Mary Lavin—they are not a group, but people dispersed, neglected and isolated in the preoccupation with bread and butter politics that followed the Treaty.

In 1923 the Revival was in its last phase. I went to the Abbey Theatre. In these agitated times the theatre was almost empty. I don't think there were more than a dozen people when I sat up on one of the hard benches of the gallery with Lennox Robinson watching *The Countess Cathleen* and *The Showing Up of Blanco Posnet*. The theatre was cold, draughty and shabby and there was a peculiar smell which was the usual smell of Dublin, the smell of horses and the Liffey. People said the smell came from the morgue on the site of which the theatre was built. It was incredible that, years before, these plays had caused riots in the theatre—though, after all, Lennox Robinson reminded me, *Widowers' Houses*, like *Ghosts*, was banned in England. When Synge's *Playboy of the Western World* was put on there was uproar because it was said to insult the Irish people.

'Audience broke up in disorder at the word "shift"', Lady Gregory wired on the first night. The stage carpenter, a man out of 'holy Ireland', commented: 'Isn't Mr Synge the bloody old snot to write such a play'. There was a week of riots. People were sent in by the political clubs to make the play inaudible. Lady Gregory got in some undergraduates from Trinity to support the performance but they made matters worse by singing God Save the King. The play had a far worse time in Boston and Chicago for the Irish-Americans (who had paid for Sinn Fein) were far more fanatical than the Irish in Dublin.

From the beginning of the movement for an Irish theatre Yeats had stood out against political plays, because he did not want art to be abused by political propagandists. *The Playboy* was not political, but in those days everything was political in Ireland and still is. When *Blanco Posnet* was put on, the Castle authorities, who played the game of the Irish bishops for favours received, threatened

Mary Lavin

to withdraw the Abbey's patent. Lady Gregory and her friends ignored the threat and so a play which must have upset some religious susceptibilities was a success, because it had defied the Castle. Years later when O'Casey's *The Plough and the Stars* was put on there was a riot on the first night; and at odd times I have seen angry people get up and shout 'Blasphemy' and rage out of the theatre. That has changed; jokes (at any rate) at the expense of the Church are received with shouts of laughter: Saint Augustine and the Jesuits—too Romish for Ireland—are comics in Flann O'Brien's farce *The Dalkey Archives*. But between 1900 and 1925 were days of solemnity and parochial anger.

Lennox Robinson, a tall thin man, with a straying Cork voice and the long rippling nose of an educated and gentle giraffe, was to be thrown out of his job as head of the Carnegie Library because he had written a pub story about a girl who claimed to have emulated the feat of the Virgin. And even this year (1966) a school teacher, John McGahern, lost his job because his novel *The Dark* was not approved. The peasant clerics of Ireland even now have great difficulty in disguising a dedicated dislike of art and literature.

The Abbey Company was remarkable, as all the world was to know. It had a great actress in Sarah Allgood who could sing a ballad like 'I know where I'm goin'' with low mysterious tenderness or blaze to the full in an emotional part. There was Maureen Delaney who was superb as termagant or indignant domesticity and who was extraordinary as Bessy Burgess in *The Plough and the Stars*. She was able to turn that blustering old Orangewoman into a tragic figure. There was Barry Fitzgerald, so lazily rich and ripe, as his face broke into innumerable lines of merriment; there was F.J. Cormick who could range from the austere to the quick-witted Dublin comic, who could play the saint, the corner boy, the dingy clerk or the Gaelic hero and whose movements were so neat and whose insinuations so subtle. I doubt if anyone played the common rain-coated Dubliner of the bars so perfectly. I pick up an old play bill. I can still hear their voices: Shelah Richards, the quintessential young Dublin girl, decorous yet gay; the severe romantic, passionate Ria Mooney who could astonish with her tongue and yet intone the lines of Synge. Arthur Sheilds, Eileen Crowe, Eric Gorman. I believe Michael Scott, the architect, appeared at the Abbey. I mention names I remember—there are many others I have forgotten—because their talents delighted audiences all over the English-speaking world. They were able to pass from *The Countess Cathleen* to *Riders to the Sea* or to Lady Gregory's

Michael MacLiammoir

14

Spreading the News, from *Kathleen ni Houlihan*—a play that used to freeze my blood for here indeed was a revenant—to the middle-class comedies of life in Cork or Dublin, from Shaw to O'Casey; and I have seen them in O'Neill, Strindberg and Molière. The Abbey was poor, its productions were simple, for the company had only a job lot of scenery, but these actors and actresses, who came out of shops and offices and not out of drama schools, were natural actors. And when they had rollicking old-fashioned satires like *General John Regan* or *Thompson in Tir na nog* they went through them as fast as a jig. The Abbey awakened Dublin. They certainly awakened me and I am grateful to them.

Of the Abbey, L. A. G. Strong wrote:

> *In this Theatre they has plays*
> *On us, and high-up people comes*
> *And pays to see things play in here*
> *They'd scut and run from in the slums.*

In 1923 Sean O'Casey was the new master. He had never been in England. He had scarcely been out of Dublin those days. He lived in a dilapidated tenement in the North Circular Road, where the glass of the fanlight over the door was smashed. Several windows of the house had gone too. The doorway was cluttered with children. He has described such a house in *Inishfallen Fare Thee Well:*

There were the houses, too—a long, lurching row of discontented incurables, smirched with the age-long marks of ague, fever, cancer and consumption, the soured tears of little children and the sighs of the disappointed newly married girls. The doors were scarred with time's spit and anger's hasty knocking; the pillars by their sides were shaky, their stuccoed bloom long since peeled away, and they looked like crutches keeping the trembling doors standing on their palsied feet.

He lived in a ground-floor room which had not much more than an unmade bed, a couple of tables and his books. Typical of slum rooms at that time, it was lit by an oil lamp. (Exactly this scene was reproduced by the Abbey Theatre when they put on his first play *The Shadow of a Gunman.*) There was a once fine but now damaged eighteenth-century fireplace, with a fire of cheap coal mixed with dust smouldering there and there was that sound which brings back the old Ireland: the singing of a kettle on the hob. I remember he told me he could remember the time when coal was 9d. a stone. Since Ireland has scarcely any coal, there is an obsessional memory of the price of it. O'Casey was an eager yet

Patrick Kavanagh

withdrawn and suspicious eccentric; he wore his cap in the house. He was one more example of the Irish predicament. He had been a labourer but (odd for this class) he was a Protestant and a Gaelic speaker: the Gaelic League did an enormous amount for the education of the poorer classes in the Ireland of his generation, far more than the wretched Irish schools did for them. Other writers who came from humble stock—Sean O'Faolain and Frank O'Connor—have described these voluntary groups which became like university reading groups. One of the natural effects of the revival of Irish was to make people read English literature. The Gaelic League recovered the lost consciousness of the native Irish, and revitalised the minds of the educated.

O'Casey had pinned a piece of paper on the wall, with the words 'Get On With the Bloody Play'. He was writing *The Plough and the Stars* at this time, which got him into trouble with the people who had fought in the Rising and the Troubles, for scepticism and anti-heroism had settled upon Dublin. Like all Dublin writers he was caught up in the perpetual Dublin jealousies and quarrels, for success is not easily forgiven. He was pursued by threats and eventually left Dublin in a rage and never returned. This was a disaster for his talent. He was one of the many for whom the powerful Dublin spell is necessary. The Irish writer works best in his own country, but his countrymen are his worst enemies and he can succeed only outside it, either in England or America. O'Casey preached unity in Ireland at a time when there was, as yet, no feeling for unity. There was nothing of the playboy character or the stage Irishman in O'Casey as there was in Brendan Behan, who came from the same world and who, a generation later, picked up a lot of his material from O'Casey and Frank O'Connor. Behan was an astonishing collector or anthologiser of well-known Dublin stories and was popular because he was a roaring personality. His drunken misadventures delighted the public. You've only to see a drunk in the streets to hear the taxi drivers evoke the rolling and blaspheming figure of Brendan, who has become, in the Celtic fashion—for the Welsh do the same—a giant and a myth. There is a general tendency to giantism in Dublin talk, just as there is in Wales.

Yeats had come back from England and was established in Merrion Square where the grand houses were still in private occupation, and not chopped up into offices as they are today. When I went to see him the door was on the chain and the barrel of a gun appeared as the door was opened. Yeats had become a Senator and the Republicans were killing Senators, so he had a guard who used

Doorway, Merrion Square

16

the ground-floor dining room with its Blake drawings as a guardroom. Yeats had taken to reading detective novels and he used to read them sometimes to the guard in order, he said, to train them in their profession.

Before I came to Dublin I had never met a great or famous person, though I had once seen G. K. Chesterton fast asleep over a bottle of wine in a London restaurant. Dublin had many great men and was full of people who knew them familiarly; this is one of the characteristics of the easy-going city. I had the ineffable experience of seeing the beautiful Mrs Yeats riding a bicycle in St Stephen's Green, of seeing the large, tweeded, bearded figure of AE going next door but one to the Yeats's, up the stairs to the offices of the *Irish Statesman,* squeezing a bunch of wallflowers in his big hands. To me these persons seemed to be beings from another world, and over forty years later I still have this impression of certain Irish people. They are real enough, yet have the faculty of vanishing into their own eyes. Yeats was famous for studiously creating a vanishing effect. Tall, with thick soft grey hair finely rumpled, a dandy with negligence in collar and tie and with the black ribbon dangling from the glasses on a short, pale and prescient nose—not long enough to be Roman, not sharp enough to be a beak—he came to meet one, a big ring on his finger, and the nearer he got the further away he seemed to float. His air was bird-like, suggesting at once one of the notable swans of Coole and an exalted blindness.

What did he say? I have scarcely any recollection at all. I have a memory of high windows, tall candles, books, and of a bullet hole in the window. I heard a deliberate, fervent, intoning voice which flowed over me as he walked up and down. We were in the middle of the Celtic revival. Suddenly he remembered tea. He had already had tea, but now he must make a new pot. The problem was where to empty the old tea leaves. It was a beautiful pot and he walked about the room with his short, aesthete's steps, carrying it in his hand. It came spout foremost towards me, retired to the book cases, waved in the air. I invented the belief that it was Rockingham and I was alarmed for it. Suddenly he went to the Georgian window, opened it and swooshed the tea leaves into Merrion Square, for all I knew on the heads of Gogarty, AE, Lady Gregory, James Stephens— who might have popped over from the Library or the Museum. They were China tea leaves, scented.

I do remember, now, one thing he said, for I had got up the courage to say a word about Shaw's socialist principles. The effect on Yeats was splendid. He

Sean O'Faolain

stopped with the teapot now full, waving it with indignation and contempt. Shaw had no principles, socialist or otherwise, he said. He was a destroyer. He was like reckless and destructive forked lightning, that lit up a landscape, might be interesting for what it revealed or distorted, but was not interesting in itself. Afterwards Yeats took me to the Senate: he was proud of being a Senator. On the way, he suddenly leaned on my shoulder while he lifted a foot, took off his shoe and shook a stone out of it. I left him, semi-conscious. Once or twice I was allowed to sit with him and AE, drinking a large goblet full of vermouth and hearing them wrangle about Fascism and d'Annunzio. AE had a way of lifting a poker and scraping the soot off Yeats's fireplace as he argued.

I often heard Yeats speak in Ireland's first Senate. Unlike the existing body, it was distinguished. This was not because of the Anglo-Irish element, but because what is discussed in revolutionary times is always fundamental. Yeats was both a practical man and a fighter. He was, of course, no democrat. He was, like every Irishman (in my belief), a reactionary: the deepest desire goes back to some imagined heroic age though it is not the desire to see such an age return. But it would seem to them pragmatic, materialistic and despicable not to act *as if* that were possible. I have often heard the complaint that the real tragedy of Ireland was that it never had a genuine aristocracy; and the speaker has somehow conveyed that he could, with any luck, have provided it. The trouble is that 'giants' and 'heroes' are not aristocratic: the concept called aristocracy is social and that, historically, has had little appeal to the Irish mind.

One could always follow Yeats's talk for he had an excellent narrative gift and what he said was, for the moment, dramatic and exact to the ear. He had the coolness of the best story tellers. I don't think I ever understood or tried to understand what AE said—except possibly about co-operative farming—for his talk simply drowned me. He worked next door but one to Yeats, sitting at a desk, effusive among his papers, in a room decorated with theosophical paintings which dazzled like some yellow sunset. One image, one idea, followed another, with Ruskinian mellifluousness. But he appeared—which Yeats did not—to love his listener and to raise him to his own state of beatitude. Like many people of a mystical turn he was hard-headed about politics and economics and shrewd in controversy. When he said he preferred the first-born of the coming race to the last spendour of the Gael, he had the manner of a huge, affable and self-congratulatory paterfamilias who had heard without surprise that that particular

Brendan Kennely

child had just been born. I have never seen such a generous measure of infinity poured into a single shaggy suit of Irish tweed. Again, not a word of what AE said remains with me; he was famous for the hours he would spend with nameless young writers; he took them even more seriously than they took themselves. His benevolence was almost crushing. I was astonished when he said he would publish the first short story I ever wrote in the *Irish Statesman* and was so sustained by this that when, two years later, he sent it back to me because he had not been able to 'get it in', I was enthusiastic, and have always boasted of it. Space was a constant difficulty on the paper, for it required all the exact, terse, bottle-nosed and sceptical talent of James Good, his assistant and one of the best tough journalists in Dublin, to prevent AE from spreading his leading articles over the whole paper.

The curse upon good talk is that it must evaporate. When it is recorded by machine it sounds flat; face, body and gesture are necessary, for the spell of good talk is created by the strange fact that this music should come out of an animal dressed in clothes. If one could have preserved a line or two from James Stephens, that nimble little gnome! He looked as if he might fall off the edge of his tea cup and drown, when he talked on Sundays at the Marine Hotel in Dunleary. Gogarty's talk must have been good because it pleased Mahaffy and Joyce tried to catch it, not very successfully, in the portrait of Buck Mulligan: one cannot expect one talker to report another. But Gogarty could not write his own talk or anyone else's. He is a good narrator, but when his accounts of Dublin dialogue are put on the page in books like *As I Was Going Down Sackville Street*, they are laboured. Yet laboured he could hardly have been in real life. Of course his malice will live, like that line about Dublin being 'stupefied by the Celtic chloroform'. And some of those speeches in the Senate in which he seems to be slithering down the slates recall the savage moments of Dublin bitterness. There is his attack on de Valera when he abolished the Senate:

The popular President has the strongest bodyguard that any man in this country had, except Lynchehauen, and I mention Lynchehauen because he turned on the hand that fed him and put his benefactor on a hot seat. History repeats itself and we are at a moment in Irish history....

Protests that it was improper to compare the President to a criminal! But in Irish debates nothing is withdrawn without making things worse:

Tinker girl (nowadays known as itinerant)

I have the greatest pleasure in withdrawing any comparison between the criminal Lynchehauen and President de Valera. I was only comparing the strength of their bodyguards, but I will alter it and say that the President is the greatest national fiasco since Jem Roche.

Jem Roche was a heavyweight boxer who was knocked out in 1908 in eighty-eight seconds. De Valera has handsomely survived these scurrilities: he is now the nation's stern, retired headmaster and old boys speak affectionately of his dignified use of the cane and collect lovingly the hairs he has split. He has been worshipped and vilified. I have often listened to discussions about his hold on the Irish mind, even on those who hate him; only President Kennedy, for special reasons, could have supplanted the image of de Valera in the mind. It is (I think) the dour and passionate grammarian of unchanging mind who has captivated a people within whose lively voices one instantly recognises the pervading tone of the melancholy pedant.

I left Dublin in 1926 and I left there, as all travellers do in every country they visit, a dump of illusions, in my case the illusions of youth. Not for twenty years did I make the dangerous decision to revisit them. And not for another twenty years did I make the even more dangerous decision to show my papers to my old Irish schoolmaster.

Jammet's

II

This city that looks more like London than any other in the British Isles is also the most foreign, the capital of a foreign country: Cork and Galway men often hold it to be foreign to Ireland itself. They also speak of each other as if they belonged to foreign tribes. We have to repeat the word of Conor Cruise O'Brien in *Writers and Politics* and speak of Dublin as a place entangled in the Irish predicament: foreign and not foreign. Another keyword is 'perplexity'.

If not foreign, Dublin is haunted by foreignness. The Londonish appearance and common language deceive us. A lady goes into one of the Baggot Street post offices, leans over the counter, plucks the post mistress by the sleeve and whispers. What can her secret be? 'Could I have a fivepenny stamp?' she is saying. In the chemist's another lady whispers, furtively, as if she were asking for the 'pill'. No, she desires a toothbrush! You ask the whereabouts of a friend: 'I have no treasonable information' is the reply: to savour humorously the remote idea of a possible treason is a private delight. There is a special vanity in the suggestion that they have pulled your leg and that you have not known it: naturally, you pretend to have been deceived. Whispers everywhere. You have entered a secret society. In offices and shops a clear, outspoken voice shocks; it is not only rude. It sounds peremptory: worse still you have said what you think when it would be better to leave the matter a mystery. There is also safety in comedy. Like the Jews and almost as much scattered over the world, the Irish are one of the world's great secret societies, a race long before they are a nation. This is foreign enough and so is the careful, almost pedantic English; so is the attention to the beauties and acrimonies of grammar and the inflexions of voice. But these are not the main foreign aspects I am thinking of. In France, Holland, Italy, Scandinavia, even—though less certainly—in Germany, we look into one another's faces and something of the continuous Western European experience holds us together. In Ireland, as in Spain or the Slavonic countries, it is not quite like that. The Romans never set foot in Ireland. Early Irish Christianity was monastic rather than episcopal; if the great formative historical movements of Europe—the Renaissance, Reformation, the French and

Old House of Lords, Bank of Ireland

industrial revolutions—ever touched Ireland, they were imported against the country's will.

The resemblances between the Irish and the non-Western Europeans are worth bearing in mind, even if the differences are large. There is an Irish claim that Spanish blood came in by the shipwrecked Spaniards of the Armada and in modern times the people of Galway have indulged the fantasy by calling an old gate the Spanish Arch; but most of the Spaniards who got ashore were massacred by the inhabitants who, in those days, were exceptionally loyal to the British. If there is a racial contact it is the remote but more suggestive one with Galicia: this Biscayan province, misty and gale-ridden, is populated by a cunning, thrifty, disputatious and dreamy people who are subject to long fits of despondency and self-laceration in the Irish manner. They play a sort of bagpipes and sing sad and pretty ballads. They are notoriously evasive. General Franco is a typical Gallegan, pious, intensely domestic and with a mind as impenetrable if not as word-preoccupied as de Valera's. The Gallegans are old Celts and have dreams of an independence lost when the Romans came. The modern resemblances with Spain are different: a Catholicism more papist than the Pope's, or rather to the right of the Holy Father; a shared intransigence, lazy but illiberal. The individual feels he is more than society. He is non-intellectual, keeps education strictly in clerical hands, feels himself to be outside Europe, is puritanical and given to vacancy of mind. ('Vacant hilarity' was Goldsmith's description of the simple ideal of unpreoccupied pleasure, and Goldsmith was Irish.)

This vacancy enables the Irishman, like the Spaniard, to muse or reflect on an inner life, from minute to minute; this musing is not thoughtful but is withdrawn. In Ireland the interest of the human face is that it is the face of an inturned mind. The Spanish mind is harder; and, in fact, the Spaniards are far better psychologists, in their mysticism, than the Irish.

As for the Russian echoes, these arise partly from the trauma of the land-owner-peasant relationship, the gift of lying, the masochistic response to authority and (as in the Spanish comparison) with the emotional prominence of personality. The heroic patriot and the 'stage Irishman' are the product of the cult. In an outstanding Irish writer, like Mary Lavin, the genius is very close to the Russian; there are Irish Oblomovs; there are Golovlyov families; in the Dublin offices and pubs—those homes of unfulfilled promises and peculiar spiders' webs of contact and back-door influence—there is something in common between

Russian 'broadness' and Irish charity; an instinctive feeling that success is unacceptable and must be torn down.

These remarks are, admittedly, based on the literary delusion that there is such a person as the generic Irish person. How can they apply to the go-getting barmen of the pub opposite, the professor of economics round the corner, the two bus inspectors whom I've twice caught arguing about 'the principle' governing their schedules while they held up the departure of the bus, the drunken actor who staggers across the road, the taxi drivers who unfailingly get the last word and who in true hip fashion say the police are getting 'dicey', the prim girl from Blackrock? The top executive, the agnostic reformer, the busy architect, the sheepish major, the dour boys in the hardware shop and the bare-legged beggar woman with the long red hair who posts herself near the Hibernian—how do they fit in? And yet Irishmen do subscribe, compulsively and fanatically, to the idea of the generic person. At any Dublin party you soon run into the national identification parade. Irish, yes; but of what kind? They will tell you instantly who is the child of a mixed marriage. They will know whether you are a Celt, Gael, Norseman, mixture of Norse and Gael, Norman, Anglo-Norman, Norman, Welsh Norman—these being called 'old English'—or lapsed 'bad English', an ancient race. Who stood where at the Reformation? Who 'turned' from one religion to another? You can have Elizabethans, Jacobites, Williamites, Cromwellians, lowland Scot, Huguenot French and the Anglo-Irish as distinct from the 'native' Irish. And, of course, there are the Irish-Americans.

These problems of identity are a matter of belligerence and melancholy; those easily excitable eyes conceal a morbid wariness.

There are also aspects of foreign appearance in the city. The quays of the Liffey do recall (but in a decaying mournful way) the quays of the Seine. The Dubliner likes to feel a bit French; in religion he is certainly Jansenist. Historically, the French have always let him down. It is an important part of the Irish dilemma that England, Ireland's great enemy, has been more reliable than her foreign friends. The superb Dublin Bay can be called Neapolitan and there are streets and houses in Dalkey and Killiney with Italian names. The Sugar Loaf mountains are like damped-down, bracken-covered volcanoes. Politically (we must constantly remind ourselves) the Irish Republic is a new country, only slightly older than the Russian satellites: the closest analogy is Czechoslovakia and Dublin has something of modern Prague, where the noble vestiges of the

Custom House

Austro-Hungarian Empire dominate a city now taken over by the Czech peasantry, a talented people, but with less style than their one-time foreign rulers, just as all that is fine architecturally in Dublin is English or of the English connection. The Irish have their tenuous link with Europe through the English and the continental experience of the Irish priesthood. One of the minor diversions of Dublin life is to take tea at Dunleary and from the terrace of an hotel, to watch the mail steamer come in from Holyhead. It makes Dubliners feel both near to the outside world and far from it. One of the half-sad pleasures is to see the mail boat go off. For Ireland is abroad, a country of greetings but of hundreds of years of goodbyes. You begin to think that your large early Victorian room in Dublin has only three walls to it; and that where the fourth wall should be, there is rain, air, space, whispering and the chaos of myth. You will often feel in Dublin that you have landed neither in time nor place. This is felt not only by other British peoples, but even more by the astonished French and Italians.

But there is a deeper foreignness than those I have just mentioned. You feel it when, coming in by sea, you see the Wicklow Hills appearing out of the water—pig-backs George Moore called them in one of his inapt Frenchified phrases—like some sportive and romantic dream. Scarcely peopled, bluish, violet or bog-brown, red or green with bracken according to the season, golden or grassy, the Wicklow Hills change their folds at every stroke of light or cloud shadow that passes rapidly over them. The names of the hills announce the mixture of native and foreign: Djouce and Mallaghcleevaun pair with War Hill and Featherbed; Lugnaquilla with Duff and Sally Gap. Seeing them at sunset the approaching stranger ceases to live on earth. He feels his mind to be dissolving, for where other mountainy coasts, especially in the Mediterranean, become more definite, this one is never stable. Anglo-Saxons need to be on guard at such hours, in such a country and (I gather from their writings) so do many Irishmen: the Celtic twilight was not entirely a literary hour. It is as well to keep in the back of one's mind that Dublin was always an enclave or citadel with a well-founded fear of the Celts or Gaelic raiders coming down from the hills. The thin military road across them built at the end of the 18th century is a sign that English Dublin was always at odds with wilder Ireland.

But to fly into Dublin from Europe is even more suggestive. Americans may miss this sensation for after their transatlantic flight they will feel they are homing on another continent at last. They are not. The European, going westward, has the truer impression. He is going out to the tattered fringes where Europe is breaking up. There is startling evidence in the sky and it is the sky that rules Irish life. As the plane burns through the air over the coast, we realise we are far out from Europe, in a distance that is more than map-miles or flying-time. We are looking down at a windy island rocking among the Atlantic isotherms and isobars, the sport of meteorology, a place shaped by weather. We are passing through half a dozen skies, moving at different wind speeds. It is true that one can come in through frisky blue skies, or skies enamelled, Italianate and eventless; or one can drop into Ireland through a ceiling as grey as an army blanket. But the usual thing is some sort of variation of chaos. I have sighted perhaps one small beam of cloud, dropped low from higher bodies, and lying sick and white over the water, as the plane makes its northward turn over Arklow or Wicklow. And, in these moments, the country looks wan and exhausted. You feel already an exhaustion rising into the air to meet you. You reach for the whiskey flask. Those wan sick clouds, only a few hundred feet above the earth, might be damp souls of little value leaving bodies that cannot care. Yet a day or two, even an hour or two later, you could be flying into theatrical anarchy, swinging from one bizarre piece of breaking-up vapour to another. Over Howth there may be little cherubic puffs of white, while a few miles across the bay, Dublin itself is under a black umbrella from one side of which yellow rain is guttering down, while at the other there is an explosion of sunshine and sailor blue. Flat white clouds lie about as if they had been dropped by accident in the south; south-west a pile of cumulus is on the boil, to the north there is a terrifying, polished wall of motionless slate, while westward, a chain of hilarious wisps race along the tops of the hills like the torn ghosts of greyhounds. You are out, as I say, in the Atlantic, where the weather is made and thrown in your European face. You have arrived at the beginning or the end of creation. You are liable to feel that you are not anywhere on earth but are being whirled about in Time and Light and strangeness. 'Like Berkeley', Aarland Ussher writes in *The Face and Mind of Ireland*, 'he (the Irishman) knows that the material world is a trick unwearyingly repeated, of that very old Gaelic magician, the light, and that truth must be both nearer and farther from us than the sun.'

But against ourselves and against Berkeley one has to put the words of Thomas Davis, poet rebel of the unfortunate Young Ireland movement of 1848. He was half-English:

This country of ours is no sandbank, thrown up by some recent caprice of earth. It is an ancient land, honoured by the archives of civilisation, traceable into antiquity by its piety, its valour, and its sufferings. Every great European race has sent its stream to the river of Irish mind: if we lived influenced by wind and sun and tree, and not by passions and deeds of the past, we are a thriftless and hopeless People.

But as a footnote to Davis one has to put Larry Doyle's speech in Shaw's *John Bull's Other Island*. The climate is different here (he tells John Bull).

You've no such colours in the sky, no such lure in the distances, no such sadness in the evenings.... An Irishman's imagination never lets him alone, never convinces him, never satisfies him; but it makes him that he can't face reality, nor deal with it nor handle nor conquer it: he can only sneer at them that do.

You come in on the tarmac at Dublin. You are on the earth and find yet another Ireland, haunted still, for it will always be haunted, but no longer Shaw's, or Davis's, or Berkeley's. Dublin is no longer Yeats's city, no longer Anglo-Irish, not even the city of Sinn Fein. No longer what one had read or known.

Ballad singer

26

III

Dublin is a capital city and looks like one. It is the capital of what is now the Irish Republic, but the independent and republican phases are so short—forty years compared with, say, 900 years of first clan or tribal and then colonial history—that the place is both less and more than it seems. One is confused by double-vision and half-shades. It is the capital of a country mutilated by an artificial boundary, and is considerably larger than industrial Belfast, the capital of Northern Ireland. Dublin is not mainly an industrial city. It has always been the centre of administration and government; it was for hundreds of years a viceregal court. I have said the place is more and less than it seems: the more lies first in the international fame it had during the struggle with England; secondly—and most important of all—in the personality of its inhabitants. But now we think of the Republic as a nation and a new one, we find that it is small. It is under half the size of England and Wales and it has approximately one fifteenth of the population, i.e. about 2,800,000 compared with forty-five million in England and Wales. The whole population of the Republic is about a third of that of London. In Great Britain, Dublin would be rather larger than Sheffield; and on the continent it is about the size of Warsaw, but smaller than Prague, Budapest or Copenhagen. At no time has the population of all Ireland, north and south, exceeded, according to estimates, eleven million. This is very much a guess and is above the population most authorities think desirable even under the best of circumstances. The Republic has had to face the fact of a population depleted by emigration. Whereas Northern Ireland is almost back to the population of 1851, the Republic fell to its lowest in 1961, according to the *Statistical Abstract of 1964;* in the present year, at a pause in the five-year boom, the decline seems to be arrested. The fact is that smaller, industrialised Northern Ireland ruled from Belfast and London has more than twice the density of population of the south. The Republic lacks many of the important raw materials of industry, but has energetically made a strong industrial beginning; its real wealth comes from agriculture and also tourism (which scarcely exists in the north). Great Britain is overwhelmingly its most important market. The natural increase in population

Mods, Fitzwilliam Square

is the highest since the 70's, but to keep young Irish men and women in Ireland is extremely difficult; they leave for England where wages are high and the services of social welfare generous. The average income per head in the Republic is £220; in the richest English-speaking countries it is £900. In the shops and offices of Dublin you hear every day the young people arguing about the advantages their brothers and sisters have in England. Some find English life too hectic. Others find it 'wicked'. Some say it is worth it, others say not. The planes and boats are crowded with people who try their luck or philander with the idea. In the recent boom, they have at any rate had the means to go and see, for overcrowded England is hungry for labour.

In forty years Dublin life has changed fundamentally. The airport is packed with people going to New York or to the English Midlands; the link between Dublin and England has moved away from London. The ties of trade have replaced the bonds of political fascination. Your taxi driver comes from Sheffield where his Irish partner is at the moment driving: they take six-month turns in each other's countries. It helps in tax evasion. You drive through new red and white building estates; the tall television masts, well strutted because of the westerly gales, fish the sky for what they can catch of the B.B.C. The Londonish streets begin as you approach the centre. You notice that the north side is dilapidated: you count the smashed fanlights; you notice that Dublin is being pulled down or is falling down: that new flats for the poorer classes are replacing the tenements of *Juno and the Paycock*. Two appalling skyscrapers stand near O'Connell Bridge and vandals have sliced down one side of a fine Georgian street at the corner of Merrion Square. In street after street the wreckers are pulling Dublin down. 'You've come just in time', people say. 'In a few years there will be little of 18th- and 19th-century Dublin left.' The Irish have always neglected their houses. When they collapse, in the countryside, the farmer simply adds a habitation or two to the ruin. Some say they are not natural builders. Traditionally the early Irish lived in forts and huts and they thought chiefly of destroying each other's encampments. There is little sense of the *civis* and no pride in it. They have a deep hatred of cities. Others say that the lack of interest or taste in building is due to poverty; yet others, that the Irish peasant—and it is his descendant who now dominates Dublin life—is as frugal as the French, and prefers to save his money rather than put it into building; and indeed, it is generally said that to 'save Dublin' is far beyond their purses. The modern Dubliner loves to pitch a

Right
Chambermaids

Next two pages
Old Dublin, Christchurch

28

fanciful tale of mushrooms as big as umbrellas growing behind the Georgian panelling; for there is excitement at the thought of comic disaster. In a short-sighted way Dubliners are indeed realists. Sites rise in value, rents go up; why not pull down and acquire what we all dream of nowadays: capital? It has to be admitted that a lot of Dublin is very shaky; it is built on bog. Four decent houses, built in 1840, opposite where I am living, are likely to fall down soon. Their walls are splitting; their windows are slipping out of shape.

But, despite the losses and the forebodings, an immense part of this little city of 600,000 people retains its Georgian and early-Victorian character. Except for the lack of smoke—for there is little industry to poison the air and take the freshness out of the colour of brick face or human face—Dublin still has a Dickensian appearance and especially as Cruickshank might see it. The difference between Dickensian Dublin and Dickensian London lies in the fact that Dublin was hardly touched by the industrial revolution. The foreignness is of time: Dubliners, whatever their new traits, never quite lose the pre-industrial peaceableness. As I say, the freedom from smoke has helped. The wind, the damp, the sea-softness, has freshened the faces; complexions pink and crimson abound. The crimson ones look either violent or placid; the ivory skins give a satanic pallor to the darker-haired. The human faces in the mass are commonplace and there are a lot of big faces with shrunken or small faces set in the middle of them— the double face, one containing the outer, the other the inner life, is very general— but the exceptional types and beautiful ones are numerous. Celt, Norse and Norman can be plausibly guessed. From what racial origins do the fine long noses, the short button noses and the famous long upper lip derive? But all the faces are double, either because of that little face, as nervous as a watch; or (more often) because Irish faces are masked, the moment the man or woman speaks.

Here is our difficulty—and this is why I have spoken of Dickens. The English face is also masked. The mask, in our case, is the public persona which we quickly learn because of the importance we give to the demands and influence of society. The Irish make little of the obligations of society; the face, with them, is masked by the policy of instant pleasing. For these passers-by belong not to society but to kith and kin. Within their family selves they live a life full of fantasy and talk, laughter and hate, outward gaiety, inner suspicion. The comedy of character in Dickens rises from the ludicrous condition of a man in the full pomp of public

Seamstress

persona, who cannot restrain foolish items of his private, inner life from bursting out; think of Sapsea, Pecksniff or Micawber. Dickens would have found an *out-wardly* Dickensian Dublin, but he would have been in the difficulty of creating Pecksniffs and Micawbers who disguise the reality within. The comic in Dickens is an inverted poetry; in Ireland it is a matter of rapid military tactics. The purpose in all the comedy one comes across in Dublin—but one comes across more solemnity than comedy nowadays—is to hide the self from vulgar definition; there is a mixed desire to ingratiate and flatter with an apparent sympathy and yet to hold something back, so as to be sure to win. One of the pleasures of Dublin life is that it never allows you the last word; the Dubliner listens to half your sentence, guesses the rest and caps it. This is pleasure because it contains half the art of story telling.

But there *is* a Dickensian Dublin because of the survival of much that is early-Victorian both to look at and in social tone; Sam Weller would not have been lost there, nor any Cockney. The wits match. You could create another Dickens from the hall porters, chambermaids, cab drivers, old soldiers, innocent girls, genteel landladies, mad aunts and the tetchy or rosy lawyers of Dublin; Victorianism has preserved them. Mayhew would have thrived as a reporter of the north side and the Coombe. South Dublin looks like Bloomsbury or the Inns of Court and is as deeply professional. Other Victorians would have fitted in: Thackeray and Trollope easily; but Carlyle not, though his rhetoric was half-Gaelic, for Carlyle preached work and, as a young Irish acquaintance tells me, work is felt to 'pollute'. But Thackeray's raffish ex-colonialism and Trollope's fox-hunting were fitting to the place; George Eliot would have failed. Emily Brontë could have belonged, but not Jane Austen; and almost none of the English Victorian poets, except perhaps Clough. I make these English literary comments not only because I have a literary bent and indeed think it is the novelists and poets who tell us most, but because the Victorian age which finally disappeared in England in the 1930's has lingered on in Dublin. One has to reckon on the time lag created by the Irish Sea. So the pace is leisurely; the gentility, the accent of refinement and the snobbery, very pronounced in the 1920's, still exist, though the Victorian houses have been broken up into flatlets. Especially the Victorian nicety has survived in the manners formed by the proprieties of family life. Although Dublin is easy-going it is easily shockable; its negligences do not drive out a decorous sense of the proper thing. The broth of

Lord Moyne

a boy is a bit of a snob; the broth of a girl is prim. Each person is conscious of his family's connections, especially in relation to Irish history—in this there is a similarity with all colonial societies; it is strong in New Englanders—and, of course, every person (and even a lot of places) are thought of as Protestant or Catholic. It is astonishing to see how watchful Dubliners are of each other. This is said to be because Dublin is a village where everyone knows everyone else; certainly a rural ethos prevails. Every word uttered in the pub or at dinner will be repeated and added to; so that one is living on a web of gossip, usually with a malicious edge to it; you can see your friends eagerly alert for it and you know they are teasing it out of you. Malice they love. It keeps their gifts alive, establishes their distinction, and sharpens what they most care for: their personality. You would not dare to ask two or three Dubliners to dinner without telling them who was going to be there. The place is full of enemies and non-speakers. And you are most carefully told, in turn, whom you will meet. This may lead to unending delicacies of offence if you meet one of the guests in the meantime. Victorian euphemisms like the 'premature' and the 'inconvenient' make a refined return to your mind.

Public relations

IV

Dublin is a spacious capital, ventilated by streets that are wider than most others in the British Isles—a Commission for Making Wide and Convenient Streets was set up in the mid-18th century: O'Connell Street is a hundred and fifty-four feet wide, Westmoreland Street ninety-six, Baggot Street a hundred, Gardiner Street a hundred; these house frontages are frequently thirty or thirty-two feet long and the depth of the plots is much longer than London plots are. The important streets, in this decisive period, were 450 feet apart and allowed for those long and seemingly endless laneways or mews in between, and for huge gardens which give the grace of nature to the urban scene. Dublin might have been built out of the poetry of Pope. The wild or sleepy airs of the sea and mountain blow freely in the streets. A circular road surrounds the city and a canal, also, which (at any rate, on the south side) creates a grateful promenade under the trees. A sense of the careless, reflective life, of innate rather than forced or crowded elegance is constant. It is no surprise to read that Patrick Kavanagh experienced a poetic rebirth after a walk along the brimming, windy canal where the swans twirl from Baggot Street to Portobello or that Parsons' Bookshop by the water at Baggot Street Bridge should have become a gathering place for writers on Saturday afternoons.

> *Leafy-with-love banks and the green waters of the canal*
> *Pouring redemption for me, that I do*
> *The will of God, wallow in the habitual, the banal,*
> *Grow with nature again as before I grew.*

Dublin's spaciousness is not splendid in the Napoleonic fashion; it is easy and encourages idleness. One of the minor sights of the city is some lonely boy picking up a golden leaf from the ground and dropping it meditatively into the Liffey or the Canal. One of the ghastly threats to Dublin is that speculating builders and car-parking barbarians talk of filling in the Canal. They are the opposite numbers of the morons who want to fill in the canals of Venice.

In the 19th century European cities went in for the grandiose. It was the

Right
Merrion Square and Upper Mount Street

Next two pages
Bank of Ireland (The Old Parliament House)

period of the Hotel de Ville and the majestic Town Hall; Dublin escaped this for political reasons. The only grand public buildings of the 19th century are the remarkable railway stations, among them the delightful château-like fantasy of Kingsbridge. The chief monuments are essentially classical: the Parliament House and the Custom House, two of the finest things in these islands, and the domed Four Courts. There are also the aristocratic mansions: Leinster House, now the seat of government, with the National Library adjacent, and until the Treaty, the home of the Royal Dublin Society; the lovely Charlemont House in Rutland Square. O'Connell Street closes at the grand façade of the Rotunda. Many of the bridges of the Liffey are fine. There is an airy metal bridge, once known as the Ha'penny Bridge (which, as I write, is in danger of being pulled down by the vandals). O'Connell Street has the Post Office which became, by accident of history, a national monument to Pearse and the men of the Easter Rising. A few houses are left of the once beautiful Mall; the rest were destroyed in the Rising and the Civil War and have been replaced by the sordid. Here the time lag has worked against Dublin: the new O'Connell Street is in the worst taste of the twenties. It is—as the word then was—Modern and of harsh and gloomy inconvenience in its interiors.

The designers of Dublin had space, and their sense of mass may strike one as too ambitious and even importunate for a poor country. The extraordinary size of Phoenix Park on its cliff up the Liffey leads one to think one is in a new county rather than a park. It would easily swallow up all the London parks and make Central Park in New York look small. The President's house, once the Viceregal Lodge, now called Aras an Uachtaran, might be a Tsar's hunting box. Here on the seemingly endless main avenue, one meets the force of the west wind and the disturbing drama of the Dublin sunsets; here too one feels how close Dublin is to something wild and pre-European. Looking back on Dublin from the cliff one sees the city not in brick but in frosty stone, its church towers are simple and war-like and the towers of its two cathedrals are harsh, though in the evenings softened by the rising damp of the bog on which Dublin is built. It is, judged by its skyline, an implacably religious city, but its belligerence is not like that of the helmeted German skylines that convey the spirit of the religious wars; the Irish anger is domestic. It suggests a family quarrel going on from generation to generation. Austerity, plainness, obduracy are the words that come to mind before these prosaic religious houses that are so indifferent to

Chapel Royal, Dublin Castle

decoration. They tell us how much of Europe Dublin has never had or indeed has never had much feeling for.

The statues of Dublin are, above all, national. There is nothing provincial about them. There are fewer than there were, for although there is an old Irish grudge that the kings of England rarely visited the country and, when they did, stayed only a short time, the royal figures have either been blown up or removed. The presence of the effigies of foreign kings and queens in an independent republic would be anomalous, yet the Irish love of the absolute seems easily to accommodate itself to anomaly. Half the Irish jokes, like the Jewish ones, come from this. One can only say that the Irish relationship to statuary, as to most other things, is personal.

There is usually a bizarre side to violence in Ireland, and in the destruction of statues the Irish have run true to form. The most notorious of these metal victims was the statue of William of Orange which once stood outside Trinity College. It celebrated the hero of the 'good old cause' and was worshipped by the victorious Orange faction, to the point of superstition; yet the statue was not exclusively a symbol of the defeat of independence. The Protestant-led Volunteer movement paraded round it in 1779 to celebrate 'the Irish harp new strung', while the church bells rang and the cannon fired salutes. But as in the case of 'the ould Orange flute', the fate of the statue was 'somewhat pathetic'—that politically cautious, evasive word 'somewhat' in the famous song is very evocative. We pause for a second to savour the wealth of Irish politeness in that qualifying adverb. If the Orange men decorated the statue with lilies, the Jacobites, Catholics and Trinity College undergraduates—the last were all Protestants in those days—vied in daubing and defacing it. Two Trinity undergraduates were fined £100 each and six months' imprisonment for 'defacing the statue of our glorious deliverer'. Soon after Emmet's rebellion in 1805, someone painted it black. It was blown up in 1836, but the pieces were gathered up and the statue was reconstructed. Daniel O'Connell, the Liberator and Catholic, tried to appease by having it done over in bronze paint. Its sufferings continued and it was finally blown up in 1929 and was smelted down in 1949; but someone apparently had gone off with the head. The site, according to Maurice Craig, from whom I take these details, is reserved for a statue of Thomas Davis, but like many Irish patriots, he has been waiting a long time for his monument—more than a hundred years—and Wolfe Tone has nothing but a poor, unlike bust in

The Royal Hospital, Kilmainham

Trinity College Library and a far too gorgeous modern portrait in Leinster House.

Other casualties are Queen Victoria, removed from the lawn of Leinster House—rather a shame because she loved Dublin and Dublin loved her when she first came over in 1849; all the Georges—but one survives in rather doughy magnificence in what was once the House of Lords and is now the Bank of Ireland, between two very fine tapestries of King Billy's victory. The pedestal of Lord Elgin stands empty in St Stephen's Green. A lazy, amiable and harmless viceroy who spent his time deep in wine and cards in the University Club, he can be held now to haunt it: for when his statue was blown up, the head is said to have been blown across the street and into the card room which was almost his permanent address.

To survive, a statue has to be on the winning side. Grattan orates opposite Trinity, Goldsmith and Burke stand within the railings. And there is Tom Moore, often insulted by writers. He and Trinity appear in Joyce's *A Portrait of the Artist*.

The grey block of Trinity on his left, set heavily on the city's ignorance like a dull stone set in a cumbrous ring, pulled his mind downward and while he was striving this way and that to free his feet from the fetters of the reformed conscience he came upon the droll statue of the national poet of Ireland.

He looked at it without anger for, though sloth of the body and of the soul crept over it like unseen vermin, over the shuffling feet and up the fold of the cloak and round the servile head, it seemed humbly conscious of its indignity.

And Patrick Kavanagh, more than a generation later, has added:

> The cowardice of Ireland is in his statue,
>   ... From under
> His coat-lapels the vermin creep as Joyce
> Noted in passing on his exile's way.

This is hard on the poet of *She is Far From the Land*, the convivial populariser of the cause of Ireland's woes in England; but one does feel the lethargy of this poetic source of the saccharined Irish tenors. There is a Dublin saying, attributed either to Gogarty or Yeats, that the capital of holy Ireland is notable for having the statues to three commanding adulterers in its main street: Parnell, Nelson and O'Connell. Of O'Connell it used to be said that you couldn't throw a stone over

Queen Victoria, for sale

a wall in Dublin without hitting one of his bastards; sometimes the wall is said to be in London. The tale is probably a libel, but it rounds off an architectural detail in the best Dublin manner. The great obelisk of the Wellington Memorial in Phoenix Park is Dublin's dominant monument, a work of assertive potency that defies the languid climate; it seems to have handed on a taste for obelisks, but unhappily at a time when slenderness rather than strength was in fashion, as if to attenuate the phallic pronouncement and to accentuate the taste for the platonic spear. Not that the phallic suggestion is altogether lost on the Dublin mind, for in his autobiography, *Round the Black Church*, Austin Clarke tells of how a fanciful Maynooth student believed that in the poorer districts of Dublin there must be some instinctive memory of ancient priapic cults which had been stirred up by the Parnell obelisk. The evidence came from a priest of the Pro-Cathedral, who had questioned a young man about a girl he had seduced in a hallway.

'What did you say she held?'

'Me parnell, Father.'

'Your what?'

The patriotic monuments to the heroes of the Easter Rising, at the Custom House or the Post Office, are in the poor convention of sentimental symbolism. Patriotism is bad for sculpture.

After the Wellington Obelisk, the happiest Dublin monument was, until 1966, Nelson's Pillar. The name was on all the Dublin buses, it gave O'Connell Street a dignity which now has almost gone. It marked the centre of Dublin, gave it gaiety and aroused ribald affection. Of course, since it was a monument to a foreign idol of Imperial power, it distressed the more sensitive patriots. There has long been a movement to pull it down, or at any rate to remove Nelson from the top; this would have been far too expensive. There was a strong movement in favour of replacing Nelson by Kennedy; others wanted the Pope or the Virgin. The matter dissolved, as so many things do in Dublin, in witticisms, anecdotes, rows, hot-headed letters to the papers and talk. If you said 'Why not sell it to the Marquis of Bath?'—a keen collector of unpopular objects—there was annoyance. If you said 'Why not blow it up?' there was black silence; in their hearts, people knew that there is always a moment in contemporary Irish life when young men think nostalgically of the explosives that are tucked away in large quantities all over the island.

Now the laughter has died down (for the second death of Nelson caused a lot

October in St Stephen's Green

36

of joking), and shame of the act is reappearing in the Irish press. One had hoped that the I.R.A.'s pride would have been satisfied by the neat shot of a sniper in the Easter Rising who, from the Post Office near by, chipped a piece off Nelson's nose; for the monument was not an alien construction. It was erected in 1808–9 and was in part the work of one of the greatest of the Irish architects, Francis Johnston, who built the Chapel Royal in Dublin Castle, designed the fine Cash Office of the Bank of Ireland, enlarged the Viceregal Lodge, the Royal Hibernian Academy, and—most important—the massive General Post Office. The Pillar (Maurice Craig has written) 'redeems O'Connell Street, potentially so beautiful, from a squalid disorder almost equal to parts of London'. The building of it was warmly supported by Dublin merchants and shippers, who were grateful because Nelson had kept the seas open for them; a little matter that remains of crucial and lasting importance in the relations between Ireland, as a whole, and Great Britain. Nelson's head, lying among the ruins, seems to have been intact—not to say distinctly conscious. There is still a pleasant picaresque episode in *Ulysses* to remind us of the peculiar effect of the Pillar on the Dublin mind.

Domestic Dublin is warm in its tints. It is brick-built and the colours of this speckled brick, ranging from sparrow-brown to pink and raw crimson, are fresh as skin. The tall Georgian windows, the pilastered doorways, the fine fanlights, have a family dignity unspoiled by extravagance or pomp. The façades rise high so that for the length of Leeson Street, Gardiner Street, Dorset Street or Harcourt Street or in Fitzwilliam Square, one is walking between high palisades, sliced off sharply at the top; one has the stagey impression of roofless, single walls. The effect is often of the unfinished and raw at the top of the houses, but the important floors are sedate. Many people find this style monotonous; but monotony is relieved by a communicated feeling—except in the very fine houses—of the friendly, even the run-down and the wild. The distances between floors—noticeable in the best houses of St Stephen's Green and the Squares—are very great and show the Dublin taste for height and scale. (Incidentally Protestants call the lovely Green Stephen's Green, the Catholics add the Saint.) For although Dublin is a low city, its chief effect upon the eye is one of verticality and height, which is due to the carefully diminished proportions of the tall narrow windows. The illusion of height is preserved also in the Victorian terraces, where the basements have been raised to ground level and the front doors are usually approached by a broad flight of twelve or fifteen steps. They are tricky because they tilt

Students, University College Dublin

outwards to drain off the rain. Sedate, cosy, ordered, private, these speckled terraces are pleasantly demure.

Many parts of the north side of Dublin and around St Patrick's are ragged and dilapidated, but there has been a really powerful drive at re-housing in these neighbourhoods. Neither the planning nor the building is attractive; there is little civic imagination; but a lot has been done to the worst slums in Europe. The familiar sight is of the shafts of timber propping up walls rising out of ruined lots. Despair and the bizarre go together, and here one feels Dublin has gone beyond caring either because money is short or the foreign sense of planning has been lost. A large part of the noble Mountjoy Square is overcrowded slum, left behind because Dublin's commerce, money and fashion have moved to the south side. The admirable Georgian Society is doing what it can to save Mountjoy Square, but the chances are not great and the speculators are busy.

In a way the stone Dublin which runs through the alleys and mews, appearing in barracks, churches, convents, hospitals, jails, railways and in long walls that seem to have been built to keep people out, is more natively Irish—in the sense of bringing rural Ireland and the strife of Irish history to the mind—than the Dublin of friendly brick. How often one is depressed by the austerity of these jail greys which, on the heavy airless days, weigh upon the mind. How unfurnished and indifferently shut in on itself (one thinks) the Irish nature must be; how much is hidden by the neglect of appearance, a neglect which ought, one had supposed, to expose the inner life.

But against this one must put the colours of the delightful, hilly Dublin suburbs along the ten miles or more of the Bay. Here terraces and graceful country houses, and the charming single-storey cottages built on the principle of the cabin—the single Irish contribution to architecture—give the coast a sparkle. Thousands of these houses, great and small, and most of them with the simple, gardened, Victorian seriousness, look out on the wide shallow strands where the thousands of gulls blow about like paper, and where the shellfish gatherers dig; or are built round the rocks of the small deep-water harbours. The sea brings its sting to the air; the green and the blue water burns. At Blackrock, at Bullock Harbour, Sea Point and Dalkey, all shaded by wind-blown beeches and the ash, the leaves of which have the dark polish of sea-light on them, the sight bemuses and is delectable. There are sunny inland hollows where the plants and bushes are rife and seemingly sub-tropical. The wind lazes, one

Mountjoy Square

seems to be safe from the present century: one wakes up to the animal life of the outdoor body. One sees why the open air, all sports, sailing, swimming, are Irish passions. At Sea Point if you stand by the Martello Tower (which Joyce shared for a time with Gogarty), at eleven o'clock on the sunny mornings in the winter, you will see ones and two's of men in their sixties drive up, undress in a hut on the rocks below and dive into the famous Forty Foot. They are the inured cold-water swimmers and were used, until fairly recently, to swim naked there. There is a strong love of what the Irish call 'manly' sports—a word which takes one back to mid-Victorian times—and there is a story that when Arthur Griffith, the Sinn Fein leader, used to rest at Gogarty's tower, he once swam the strenuous mile between Sandycove and Bullock Harbour and had to be rescued at the last minute by the surgeon.

Across the Bay, Howth rises high out of the flat isthmus that recalls the landscape of Holland and seems afloat in the sea. Here on the seaward side the fishing fleet comes into harbour. It is pleasant to walk up the long quay on one of those innocently fair Dublin mornings to the deep water where the boys are catching what they call 'pollock' and to think of Swift, the irascible pedant, complaining that the old Dublin cry of 'Herrings alive, alive here' was a lie because a fish would be dead one minute, three seconds and a half, before it was sent across the Bay. It is lovely to see the whole hill of Howth in flower in the spring. How far away one seems to be, as the lights sprinkle the Bay and some slow cattle boat goes out alone, although the cars will be driving back to Dublin half the night. How far away, too, when one listens to the ballad singers at the inn. The great crowd, filling up with Guinness, listens to the traditional airs about the martyrs, the heroes, the lonely girls; it roars to the *Ould Orange Flute* or *Kevin Barry*. It is excited by those suddenly whizzing, farcical tongue twisters, like *Finnegan's Wake*. One does not see the ragged old ballad singers in the streets nowadays—in the language of the new Irish respectability tinkers are called 'itinerants'—but ballad-making is very near the surface of the Dubliner's mind. He likes a song and can change in a moment from the clear murmuring voice of sadness to the rip-roaring. The little poem is always a little story. I never walk down the quays without remembering that little gem of Dublin life by L. A. G. Strong:

Have I a wife? Bedam I have!
But we was badly mated:

View from Joyce's tower

I hit her a great clout one night,
And now we're separated.
And mornin's, going to me work,
I meets her on the quay:
'Good mornin' to ye, ma'am!' says I,
'To hell with ye', says she.

V

Seaports are frontiers; their tone is liberal and, in a country where fanaticism has walled people in, Dublin is (for Ireland) liberal. The blood is mixed. Live-and-let-live is played as a prickly comedy. Dublin has always been a sociable city and that has turned the religious and political tension into a game of cards—but only on the surface. The periods of outrageous religious tyranny and exclusiveness have never lasted very long: tolerance and the built-in habit of getting round the law have quietly got their way. Still, an edginess or soreness about religion is certainly there. The small Protestant population has been slowly declining since 1870; but in the period of the Troubles there was naturally a sudden and large decline: in ten years, a hundred thousand Protestants left the Irish Republic; there are now only about a hundred and forty thousand left out of a total population of two million eight hundred thousand. In Dublin, they own a great deal of the commercial wealth. The claim to be an Ascendancy vanished during the 19th century and though snobbery makes many Protestants anxious to believe they have some relation with the almost vanished gentry class, they are no longer a force in the social or political life of the city. They are also an ageing group. In the first flush of political power the Catholic majority created a Catholic peasant state which was well on the way to being as exclusive as the Spanish. A sweeping censorship of books was soon established; the Senate, in which many distinguished Protestants had a voice, was abolished; and replaced eventually by a body far less distinguished; there is no divorce and birth control is legally non-existent.

There has been a reaction against this extremism in recent years. In spite of an Archbishop who appears to be in favour of religious apartheid—the Protestants and agnostics being the 'negroes'—there is a not negligible movement towards Catholic liberalism in Dublin; in the last two years the magic word 'ecumenical' had a great deal of lip service, for the Philistine and reactionary tone of the main body of Irish Catholics has been an embarrassment to them in their relations with European Catholics, and a disaster in the crucial matter of secondary and university education upon which the urgently needed modernisation depends.

As the French-Canadians discovered in 1946, they were shut out of the modern world through sticking to the educational system of the 17th century. Nearly all the Irish Catholic intellectuals I know are either lapsed or indignantly calling for reform; and this is true of the ordinary man who has woken up to the fact that his children are getting a very poor chance. Anti-intellectualism has always been an Irish difficulty—the failure of the Church to provide a moral consciousness is a favourite theme of Sean O'Faolain and other important Irish writers—but the foreigner who thinks of Ireland as priest-ridden, an island packed with seminaries, missions, monasteries and convents out of all proportion to its population, must bear in mind that the appalling political history of Ireland, which reduced the 'native' Irish to slavery and misery, made the parish priest the only friend the people had. He is a member of the family, consulted in every detail of family and social life. The Irishman is, once more, in a predicament; and is inclined as usual to make comedy out of it.

'Keeping late hours', says a Catholic acquaintance, 'is a secondary religious characteristic. If a man goes to bed late, he is a Catholic; if he goes early he is a Protestant.'

When Irish hopes were dashed at the Horse Show a few years back and an Italian won, my friend said:

'Anyway, it's been a good day for the Pope.'

A large number of Catholic students have got their priests' permission to send their sons to Protestant Trinity. There has been a Jewish Mayor of Dublin and—as some Protestants re-join Irish political life—there could very well be a Protestant one. The greatest Dublin joke, and one of the best of Jewish jokes too, is that Leopold Bloom, the great, vulgar, shabby Jewish clown and *cocu*, created by that famous lapsed pupil of the Jesuits who left Dublin in disgust—'but Belvedere College has changed since Joyce's time'—has become a secret anti-saint of the city. Dublin likes the great evasion of the laugh; it relieves one of the danger of having one's mind read and forwards the tricky business of keeping the big guns of polemic booming away while, under cover of the noise, one devotes one's continually sharpened intelligence to manoeuvre. The effort is self-consuming, for talkers are hermetically enclosed in their self-love. Yet, when the talk stops and the light goes out in the talker's face, one sees he is at once aware of his real situation. He is not so different from his sparring partners across the Channel—the day-dreaming English enclosed in their cli-

chés, the startled Welsh, the conscience-stricken Scots, who all find themselves forced to live in one another's pockets, are alike in one thing: they are frontier dwellers. It is their curse and their advantage.

I was thinking of another kind of frontier when I said that Dublin is a frontier city. It became, very early on, the point of contact with western England and Western Europe. Edward Curtis says in his *History of Ireland* that the Irish people are the oldest of any race in Europe north and west of the Alps and the only Celtic nation state left in the world. A Celtic state? Dream or reality? Reality only if one recognises that it has been mangled by its own tribal wars, by many invasions and half-conquests. A special kind of frontier spirit exists, because Ireland had the great misfortune of having been crushed but of never being thoroughly defeated. To be raided and passingly raped (as London also knew in its Danish days) is not enough.

Dublin Bay and the balmy shelter of the little Liffey made an ideal haven for the raider. The Liffey marked the first break in the mountain defence of Ireland. It set the route to the rich Irish midlands and the name of Dublin or Dark Pool refers to the dark bog waters of the Liffey. The other name Atha Cliath, refers to the ford of hurdles. The Norsemen came for cattle and the metals of Wicklow; it was a place where it paid them to stay and to stave off the continual Irish counter-attacks. Even after the defeat of the Danes at Clontarf on the north side of the Bay, the Norsemen remained, for the Irish had spent their force.

David Greene, in his lecture on Early Irish Society (edited by Myles Dillon), tells us that the Gaelic power was destroyed:

I say destroyed because, although the Scandinavians did not last long as a great political or cultural force, they effectively undermined the Gaelic system by the establishment of towns which were to remain ever after strongholds of a non-Gaelic and anti-Gaelic influence.

And Professor D. A. Binchy adds:

With the doubtful exception of Cashel, none of the large cities and towns is of native provenance; they have all been superimposed from outside upon a rural pattern of life. Even the village, which was the basis of Anglo-Saxon England, had no place here; indeed, down to the present day the isolated holding remains characteristic of the country district in Ireland and Wales in contrast to the typical groups of houses clustered round the parish church in England.

The early history of Ireland for centuries reads like the history of the Scottish border. One sees Dublin on the frontier of two cultures. The Norsemen turned

David Greene

43

Christian and built Christchurch Cathedral, but Irish research has gathered some evidence that there may have been a native church on the site. The new race of Norse mestizos were called Ostmen: the frontier spirit was established.

If only Dublin had been in the centre of Ireland (some historians have said), the country would have had unity: would it not have been destroyed in the clan wars? There is a pause and then the Normans came. At first they are called Anglo-Normans or Welsh-Normans, for they were the landless unsatisfied younger sons of the Norman families in Wales. They succeeded because they were well armed and able feudalists. Norman Ireland ultimately failed because there were not enough Normans, they quarrelled among themselves. But they intermarried with the Irish and out of this union came the two great Anglo-Norman families: the Geraldines of Kildare (afterwards Dukes of Leinster), and the Butlers of Kilkenny (afterwards Dukes of Ormonde). When the tourist goes into St Patrick's, the guide tells the well-known story of how the rival parties met to make peace there. Archers left outside the meeting became restive and passed the time in the old schoolboy pastime of shooting things at the ceiling. The things were arrows. Treachery was suspected. And the only way to calm the suspicious negotiators was to cut a hole in the door and make them shake hands through it. The peace did not last. The story is typical of medieval life anywhere in Europe; but in Ireland it is the manner of the guide that is the making of it. There is a cynical, excited relish in his voice. For two pins he would tell you he was there at the time, or at any rate feels or wishes he had been. Afterwards, one reflects that no literature has come out of the Norman attempt to set up feudalism in Ireland; in later centuries, no Shakespeare saw the material of an Irish Wars of the Roses. The reason must be that colonialists who are a small if able minority become gangsters if they are not numerous enough to create a society. And gangsterism is a frontier characteristic for colonials are beyond reach of the central power; they are free to act on their own. The conquering colonial has always felt free but he has paid for his freedom by the weakening of the morality that restrains him in his own country. The impromptu of Irish life begins here and, very likely, it is here that the cult of personality has its roots. Irish history is full of outstanding individuals who are not simply leaders but are remarkable for everything in their lives. Norman soldier becomes Irish chieftain; the conqueror falls into the habits of the conquered. In isolated parts the Norman adopted the Irish habits. Towards the end of the

Right
The Coombe

Next two pages
Christchurch Cathedral

13th century laws were passed against 'degenerate Englishmen' who 'attire themselves in Irish garments and having their heads half shaven grow and extend the hairs from the back of the head … conforming themselves to the Irish as well in garb as in countenance'.

Although King John subdued his Anglo-Norman vassals and made them swear to keep English law, this meant, as it always does in colonial practice, that there was one law for the colonists and no law, except where native rule survived, for the native Irish. Feudalism made them serfs.

'The weakness of feudalism everywhere', says J. C. Beckett in his *Short History of Ireland*, 'was that the force of royal justice depended mainly on the vigour and ability of the King, and if royal justice was weak the barons were almost compelled to settle their differences by war. This is what happened from time to time in every country settled by the Normans—England, southern Italy, Palestine; but in Ireland it became almost the normal state of affairs.'

The ambiguous relation of Dublin to the warring Ireland on the other side of the Wicklow Hills was its strength. In each colonial wave that followed, in the Elizabethan, the Cromwellian and Williamite periods, the city's ruling interests and politics tied it to England, yet those who looked back to England for their advantage and defence had a divided loyalty. Colonists oppress but they are the first to see themselves as independent of the mother country. Within the Pale, along the eastward coast of seaports with Dublin as their centre, they were strong. They were enriched by trade. If there was anything resembling a Court, Dublin became the place for it and its idea was inspired, not by the North of England, which was nearest to it, but by London which was the centre of power. But London was a great city when Dublin was hardly more than a strong point with a small collection of warehouses and monastic buildings. The area of London within the walls was two thirds of a square mile in the Middle Ages; the area of Dublin was one ninth of a square mile. It was not yet a capital and although it had two cathedrals it was ruinous and the Castle was called the worst in Europe. (Two Protestant cathedrals built for the best of Irish reasons: a quarrel. Trinity College had been founded by Elizabeth. In 1668 a Frenchman admired the rare books in the library.) The population was 9,000; London already numbered its hundreds of thousands and had burst its walls. The vast difference makes the sudden achievement of the Dublin Anglo-Irish in the late 17th and 18th centuries stupendous. From a depressing stone settlement on its

Orphanage, Dominick Street

45

little hills surrounded by bog it became a fine city, elegant, aristocratic and wealthy.

Historians like to draw a cultural trade route that approximates to the Mediterranean trade route of Europe from Constantinople to Venice and Milan, over the Alps either to Paris or the Rhine, Amsterdam and to London—London being a terminal and getting the benefits of Europe late. Dublin was simply later. The Renaissance can be said to have arrived in London in 1615, after Inigo Jones had been to Italy; it came to Dublin in 1662 when James, Duke of Ormonde 'stepped out of his pinnace' on to the sands of Dublin Bay.

The words come from Maurice Craig's scholarly book on Dublin. To Maurice Craig's *Dublin 1660–1810* and to Constantia Maxwell's *Dublin Under the Georges*, anyone writing about this period must owe an enormous debt—my own a shameless one. Craig's book is a monument to that most brilliant century of Irish life when the outward character of Dublin was established.

The Duke of Ormonde (writes Craig) was now 52, the ninth member of the House of Butler to hold vice-regal office, and himself an ex-viceroy. He brought back with him memories of his last departure from Dublin twelve years earlier, involved in the defeat of his royal master. He had more recent memories of the opulent grandeur of Louis XIV's Paris and of his own poverty and humiliation in the lean years of exile.

(Exile being the perennial Irish experience, whatever the Irish strain.)

He had seen in France the happy effects of the toleration of Huguenots and had learned the lesson which the French King was soon to forget. He himself had a family background which was partly Catholic, partly Protestant, matching to a nicety the country he was now to rule. Above all, he had absorbed on his travels the conception of the centralised state and the ceremonial capital.

The political history of the Ormonde—or post-Ormonde—period is not my subject. At bottom it was disgusting: the Protestant interest is based on the robbery of Catholic property and the degradation of the Catholic population— who were not all 'native' Irish—and the loyalty of the Protestant settlers to the English crown is always in question when the title to their stolen lands seems to be threatened. The Stuarts were themselves in the awkward situation of having to cozen the Cromwellian settlers whom they hated. Some Catholics got back part of their land. A Commission of Settlement was working out 'an opportunist and unstable patchwork, making a nice distinction between Cromwellian and "innocent Papist"'. In the National Library in Dublin one goes through the lists of settlers and their acreages, the claims and counter claims of a fierce and miserable story. One sees the entangled roots of the bitter Irish passion for history as genealogy, which can still crop up in Dublin conversation.

But when Ormonde set out to make Dublin splendid, the word Ascendancy had meaning. Little of the Dublin Ormonde saw now exists. St Patrick's and Christchurch are there. The churches are in Protestant hands. There are pockets known as Irish quarters. At the town's edges there are derelict monasteries and there are water mills and windmills. It recalls, in a way, another colonial settlement: early Manhattan. But soon Dublin stretches one way towards Trinity College from the Castle and in the other direction along the rambling westward-going street above the Liffey cutting through the now tumbling slums of old Dublin, passing the Guinness brewery and the Royal Hospital at Kilmainham and down across the river to the green cliffs of Phoenix Park. You sit in the cold gloom of Dublin's oldest pub, the Brazen Head, in Lower Bridge Street, depressed by the wreckage of time.

Ormonde gave the Royal Hospital at Kilmainham, which has one of the finest interiors in Ireland, and the Phoenix Park to Dublin. The name has nothing to do with the classical Phoenix: it is a corruption of the Gaelic name for a nearby spring: Fionn-Uisge. The surrounding stone wall, running on for miles, might be the progenitor of all the grey stone walls of Ireland: it was built by a swindler and often fell down. The Park itself was intended as a deer park; the descendants of the English deer are still there, giving delicacy and company to the vast, empty lengths of green. There, in the 18th century, Sir Lucius O'Trigger and other sensitive Dubliners fought their innumerable duels; there in the 19th century a First Secretary was murdered by the Invincibles; there now the Saturday hurley and football games are played and the crowds visit the Zoo.

Ormonde came of a Catholic family but, as a child, was obliged by James I to be educated as a Protestant. The conversion was complete. He was continually under attack because he was suspected of favouring the Papists. Two fantastic attempts to capture and murder him were made by one Colonel Thomas Blood, an Englishman and Cromwellian adventurer who represented Protestants who were resisting Catholic attempts to get back their lands. He captured Ormonde who was dining with the Prince of Orange, and intended personally to hang the Duke at Tyburn. The Duke fought his captors off at the gallows itself, while the rope was being fetched. These incidents are worth mentioning because, like many on other social levels in Dublin, they show how strong the habits of gangsterism or the frontier are in the colonial situation. And how lawless were the streets of the sister country. But there was also another spirit, hard-headed, bold, diplomatic, humane and deeply Irish in the last sentence of Ormonde's reply to the fanatics among his Protestant opponents. His words are quoted by Craig:

My father and mother lived and died Papists, and bred all their children so, and only I, by God's merciful providence, was educated in the true Protestant religion, from which I never swerved towards either extreme, not when it was most dangerous to profess it and most advantageous to quit it.... My brothers and sisters, though they were not very many, were very fruitful and obstinate (they will call it constant) in their way. Their fruitfulness hath spread into a large alliance, and their obstinace has made it altogether Popish.... But I am taught by nature, and also by instruction, that difference in opinion concerning matters of religion dissolves not the obligations of nature; and in conforming to this principle I own not only that I have done but that I will do my relations of that or any other persuasion all the good I can.

It is an amusing and honourable expression of the force of kinship in the Irish tradition. Alas, in less than a generation the Penal Laws were being enforced by a violent Protestant Parliament and the notorious Orange Toast was being drunk to 'the glorious, pious and immortal memory of the great and good King William; not forgetting Oliver Cromwell, who assisted in redeeming us from popery, slavery, arbitrary power, brass money and wooden shoes.... And he that won't drink this toast may a north wind blow him to the south and a west wind blow him to the east! May he have a dark night, a lee shore, a rank storm and a leaky vessel to carry him over the river Styx...' and a lot more until he is 'blown with a clean carcass to hell'. Dublin was always a city for extravagance and many a Papist must secretly have enjoyed the metaphors and have sworn to surpass them.

The population had grown to 50,000. Dublin had the attraction of a Court and of a mercantile city. It exported cattle: it imported luxury goods from England and sold them dear in the colony—again the history of early Manhattan. The persecution of the Huguenots had brought over the Dutch and Flemish weavers who built Dutch houses—one or two remain. They settled south of the Castle in what is called the Coombe and established not only their skills but their immigrant riots. The Coombe continued the tradition of violence

up to twenty years ago—'It's quietened down; they've all grown old or emigrated', is the phrase you hear now. In the 18th century, the weavers marched down upon the butchers of Ormonde Quay in savage street war. The butchers cut the leg-tendons of the weavers; the weavers hung the butchers by the jaws on their own meat hooks.

Dublin's great century had begun late, but it had begun in one of Europe's best periods of city building. The little town was to become a shadow capital. It was to have some able or beneficent viceroys: the influence of Lord Chesterfield would bless any city. It surprises me that his delightful monument has not been blown up. These men encouraged the serious interests of Anglo-Irish life. In this period the Royal Dublin Society was founded; its interests were scientific, agricultural and philosophical. It was the period of the building of Trinity College Library and the monumental façade of the University. Swift, Burke, Goldsmith and Berkeley are in the streets, and we hear the protests of Goldsmith—he always refused to drink King William's health—and in the rage of Swift begins the Protestant revolt in the struggle for Irish freedom. Goldsmith's case is even more interesting, if far less dramatic and effective, than Swift's, in what it reveals of the Anglo-Irish mind at the time. 'There he is, the poor fellow', the old fraud of a guide used to say, donkeys' years ago, his eyes watering and his testy voice going soft, when taking one to look at the array of busts in Trinity College Library. He would stop for half a tear before Goldsmith's innocent and comic face. A disastrous undergraduate, ugly, with a pointed nose—which always reminded me of the strange nose of Forrest Reid, a delightful Irish writer of my time, now I fear forgotten—loving to dress up in gaudy clothes, incoherent in talk, over-fond of cards, reckless with money, but good at playing the flute, a sweet singer of Irish ballads and a wit when he wrote. Goldsmith is the type of all that is droll and endearing. He was the son of a poor Irish farmer-clergyman from Roscommon who migrated to Kilkenny, which was an important centre of education, and he was sent as a sizar to Trinity. As a boy, he had not kept himself apart from the native Irish; nor had his teacher, a quartermaster of the British Army who was a Gaelic speaker and had a passion for Irish legends and poetry. Two cultures almost met in the minds of these odd figures; there must have been many more like them before Gaelic vanished in the early 19th century only to be revived by scholars.

Goldsmith wrote an account of Irish manners which is interesting both for

Jonathan Swift, Trinity College Library

49

its sympathies and its rationalising of the colonial dilemma; he invented for himself a paternalistic theory of the childish innocence of the native Irish and in doing so himself became an innocent. Or rather—and I have mentioned earlier his feeling for 'vacancy of mind'—a man who valued freedom from preoccupation. He appears to have believed this was a characteristic of the Irish peasantry and to have thought that the English had made this blessing possible by taking away their political rights! We see that Goldsmith's graceful, clear, personal and simple style—a style that was to become characteristic of Anglo-Irish literature which had freed itself from English sententiousness—was formed not by innocence of mind but by conflict of mind.

The Anglo-Irish had, Goldsmith said,

> superinduced over the rough English character a degree of ceremoniousness and politeness which may serve to distinguish the two nations ... the Irish protestants are ... affable, foolishly prodigal, and often not to be depended upon. This difference from their ancestors they have acquired by long conversation with the original natives, who carry their faults to a vicious extreme. The original Irish are therefore frequently found fawning, insincere, and fond of pleasure, prodigality makes them poor, and poverty makes them vicious, such are their faults, but they have national virtues to recompense these defects. They are valiant, sensible, polite and generally beautiful.

For Goldsmith, Irish men were lascivious, but the women modest. And those who have wondered about the prudery and the often mentioned sexlessness of the Irish nature, will be reminded of Berryman's *The Midnight Court*, written in the 18th century, by Goldsmith's words: 'So that if Venus were to fix a temple in any part of the world it might be here in the land of Honeys and Joys.' One wonders. Goldsmith was refused a kiss from a village girl; and indeed the above passage ends with a suggestion that it was Venus and not a real woman who was to be addressed: 'Fanned by luxuriant airs what shepherd refuses to sing or what nymph disdains to hear.'

After high place in London, Swift experienced a feeling of defeated ambition and impatience when he returned to provincial Dublin; many other Irishmen have had the same experience, but they found themselves distinctive there and —if they were caught by the passionate question of the condition of Ireland— they found greatness. The life of Berkeley is enough to show that to be in Dublin was not to be outside the European current in this century. Lord Chesterfield said that education was better in Ireland than in England at this time.

Housekeeper

Swift was at school in Kilkenny with Congreve, Berkeley and Farquhar. Swift contains the Anglo-Irish agony of the time. Ambitious and arrogant, he is caught in the dilemma which all the distinguished Irish have had to face: whether to go or to stay. His genius carried him easily to the centre of English greatness; he fought for Ireland when he failed in London. The experience of dual nationality fertilised if it also lacerated. It is true that in his Protestantism and his immediate political interests, he represented the Anglo-Irish view; he was, for example, unyielding about tithes which were a serious instrument of oppression; it may be that when he wanted Ireland to be free, he wanted this freedom for the Anglo-Irish Ascendancy alone. But the plight of the native Irish must have been present continually in his mind, influencing it as a landscape, and the direct sight of people, always influence. To his indignation was added a savagery which must perpetually have been whispered to him by the crowd. The *Modest Proposal* may have been put into his mind by the brutal butchers of Ormonde Quay. The young undergraduates of Trinity had a wild population on their doorsteps. They were wild themselves—hence the severity of university rules; they once murdered a tutor.

It is the century of fine mansions and houses. The Royal Hospital at Kilmainham was built in 1680; Burgh began to build Trinity Library in 1712. Leinster House, Charlemont House, Powerscourt House, Upper Castle Yard, the Rotunda, the Blue Coat School, the King's Inns, the Provost's House, the Custom House, some of the best bridges over the Liffey, belong to his century; and the impulse continued into the early Victorian age. There was, as indeed in England, an enlightened and distinguished practicality. Berkeley was a Bishop and a philosopher—and in philosophy the most musical of the anti-materialists—but he wrote down his famous *Queries:*

'Whether a gentleman who hath seen a little of the World, and observed how men lived elsewhere, can contentedly sit down in a cold, damp, sordid habitation, in the midst of a bleak country, inhabited by thieves and beggars.'

A question to be read beside the information that in 1730 the yearly value of the income spent by Irish absentees abroad was £621,499, which in forty years grew to a million and a quarter. Swift and Berkeley, the economist Prior, and the Molyneux brothers were all 'improvers'; Lord Cloncurry said that for wit and pleasure (though, of course, for the rich alone) Dublin life could be compared

Rotunda Chapel

with Paris. Benevolence was the ideal of the enlightened. Swift and Stella both left large sums for the building of hospitals.

A violent or irascible mob, a mercantile class getting richer, the overwhelming power of a landed aristocracy, a striking increase of amenity in city life: the eighteenth century is built on these contradictions in England, in Europe as well as in Ireland. Countries have never been so tyrannically ruled in the West: towns have never been so well planned and built anywhere since. Thomas Burgh's Library at Trinity, a classical building, in Dublin's granite that is always unfeeling to the eye, has one of the largest reading rooms in the world. Its narrow length has the effect of a cathedral aisle, in which the window embrasures might act as bookish side chapels. Craig thinks of the general shape as a mill or huge warehouse of learning, and this is well said: for one has so often the sense in Dublin that the severe buildings are made on a large scale, first because Dublin always had space, but also because, as a colonial city, it had the tradition of the 'Factory' which can hold large stores. Trinity Library is a packed store and a treasure house: it is frankly ambitious, but not pretentious, and it has little fantasy. It is one of the few massive buildings in Dublin that do not seem too massive for what they are built to contain and do not suggest—as so much of stone Dublin does—coldness and lack of intimacy. The great rectangular block is accommodated to the College. And then, a library in itself proclaims the human personality.

Trinity College was founded in 1591, in Elizabeth's time. In the Examination Hall there is a portrait of the Queen under which—one is told—it is unlucky to sit. Originally the College was built in red Dutch brick. There was no exclusion of students on religious grounds before the Charter of Charles I; and not for many generations now has there been exclusion. (A favourite joke of Dublin taxi drivers—spoken to please English visitors—is 'And there's Trinity College where you can study any bloody religion you like'—which is interchangeable with the one once offered me by a drunken jarvey: 'Do you know which is the only true bloody religion: it's the bloody Catholic religion—I had it from a priest.') The square just inside the Gate is very fine, the Victorian campanile is impressive. And there is the splendid museum in Venetian Gothic which Ruskin startled Dublin by admiring. Old tales of the riotous behaviour of undergraduates in Botany Bay, so-called because it looks like a jail hidden away, still go round; you were thought to be tough if you lived there. Placed in the centre of the city, Trinity was also thought to be dangerous for the morals of the young, but its

Trinity College Library

political distinction may owe something to its situation opposite the old Parliament House. Great patriots, men like Grattan, Tone, Emmet and Thomas Davis had only to cross the street to have their patriotism inflamed.

It is said that the chief motive for putting the Irish Parliament in Leinster House in 1922 was the Civil War. Fighting and assassination were going on in Dublin and Leinster House was well railed in and was more easily defensible. Another argument is that the old Parliament House, despite its long battles for Irish freedom, had thought chiefly of freedom for the Ascendancy settlers and not for the Irish of native stock. Yet the rebel spirit of Grattan (one would have thought) had purged whatever monstrous sins lay in the nobler building. It was 'contrived' (to use the 18th-century word) for the activity of the new genus called architects—by a brilliant young man. Edward Pearce was a cornet in the Dragoons in 1715, of English stock. One of his forebears on his father's side was James I's agent in Venice and a client of Rubens: so often in Anglo-Ireland one sees the European strain continuing through London to Dublin. As C. P. Curran says in his account of the building, the age offered power to young genius. It is surprising to us—but it was not to the men of that time—that Pearce sat in Parliament and became Surveyor General at thirty-one. Vanbrugh was Comptroller of the Board of Works in England at thirty-three. In F. G. Hall's *Bank of Ireland, 1783–1946*, which was edited by George O'Brien, the authority on Irish economic life of the 18th century, we find Curran writing:

> The acceptance of a regular style in architecture based on fixed proportions, the circulation of architectural copy books with their specimens of the orders from Palladio, Scamozzi, Serlio, Vignola, Alberti, Viola, Perrault, Le Cleri and others, and the growth of a competent body of artificers who could be relied on to carry through with exactness the models placed before them: these circumstances encouraged amateur enterprise.

And propaganda for better building was being ardently made by the Dublin intellectual societies, for when the Parliament House was being built, there was little to look at except Trinity Library and the Royal Hospital. The general taste of the buildings near Trinity was Anglo-Dutch and Hanoverian, a higgledy-piggledy of gables and feeble decoration.

The eighteenth century's spirit of improvement, its feeling for order and elegance, triumphed rapidly in Dublin. The Gardiners built up the north side. Henrietta Street—still there, but more than half slum—housed an archbishop, a bishop and four peers; and until an alderman—in the 20th century—ripped out

Trinity College, Dublin

the staircases and turned some of them into tenements, they were noble. Lady Blessington's ballroom, with its lovely Italian stucco, is now in the hands of the nuns who at any rate preserve it. There is a fine staircase at No. 9. In the other houses, you enter those vast entrance halls that are familiar in old Italian houses in Genoa and Naples and under the stained and dirty colour wash you can see the ghost of a lost grandeur, while above the poor families are crowded into one room.

But after its turn to the north side, fashionable Dublin reversed its movement and went southwards across the Liffey. Stephen's Green and Grafton Street were built. And then the Earl of Kildare built Leinster House; the Lord Mayor got his Mansion House; the Green got its great houses; the Mall was built and the astonishing Rotunda, cheerfully designed to hold a lying-in hospital, a fashionable Vauxhall and theatre on one site—one of the happiest notions a planner ever had. The Gate theatre and a cinema still keep up the genial tradition. The city had to reckon with the rakishness of its enriched settlers. Craig says:

> Immigrants who, had they stayed in England, would have behaved like normal Englishmen, found in Ireland an almost rootless society of speculators and go-getters. Many individuals adopted a violent habit of behaviour which brought them closer to the dispossessed helots than might have seemed possible.

So when we think of the fine Dublin mansions, the beautiful Italian and Irish ceilings of stucco in St Stephen's Green, in Belvedere House and in Lady Blessington's house in Henrietta Street, of the grave arguments of the Dublin Society, of Berkeley, Molyneux and of Swift and the elegancies described by Mrs Delany, we have also to think of the bucks and riotous gentlemen-hoodlums in Dublin and the Rapparees in the countryside. The two sets of delinquents complement each other. The Tories or Rapparees were the angry victims of the new landlords in the country out of whose profits Georgian Dublin was being built. Arthur Young noted their forays in his *Tour of Ireland*. They burgled and assaulted and burned and murdered in country houses. Wolfe Tone's *Journal* describes how his father's house was wrecked and how he was rescued by his brave young wife. The rakes appeared in any political disturbance from ordinary riot to massacre in the religious quarrels. The horror of the killings is unspeakable and has contributed to the view—oddly acceptable to Irish people—that the Irish have a fundamental streak of coldness and cruelty. (In literature, indeed, there are signs

85 St Stephen's Green (University College Dublin)

of a merciless and pre-Christian sense of cruelty and tragedy.) The Dublin Bucks and hoodlums, on the other hand, strike one as being English in brutality and horseplay and very similar to the people who made the London streets intolerable when Fielding was a magistrate and when the London upper class became full-bloodedly depraved. There is the example of the diabolism of the 'monks' of Medmenham. From the latter indeed the Hell Fire Club and the antics of the Ist Earl of Rosse, Buck English and Buck Whaley seem to derive. (I was brought up on the legend that the sinister little ruin on the top of the Dublin Mountains which is called the Hell Fire Club was the site of the orgies; but historians now say there is no evidence. I incline still to the legend on the general ground that what goes on in cities is nothing to what goes on in the country.) And Craig veers to this opinion when he recalls the famous experiment by which the members set fire to the club while they were in it, in order to give greater realism to the sensations of Hell. The incident would not have seemed incredible to Dostoevsky, as we can see in certain pages of *The Idiot*: Russian and Irish parallels again! The landowners were inclined to murder servants and certainly flogged the peasantry. There was a long vogue of duelling and the duellists 'blazed' in the Dublin streets and even among the crowds in Phoenix Park. To 'blaze' was indispensable. Lord Clanmorris horsewhipped a lawyer in the street. Another barrister, according to Barrington, had his 'eye saluted by a moist messenger' in the House of Commons. 'Hilt to hilt' and 'muzzle to muzzle' was a gentlemanly ideal. In 1777 the Fire-Eaters appeared. Galway issued the thirty-six commandments of duelling. There were groups of noctambulists called the pinkindindies. They 'pinked' and slashed their victims who, having lost at the gaming tables, got their money back off pedestrians. They grabbed women in the streets. They rioted in the theatre. Often the stage itself was occupied by some of the audience who walked about and interrupted the actors. In Sheridan's time, the theatres were a mixture of bear-garden and brothel. In an effort to keep the audience off the stage, iron railings were put between audience and players. Barrington—who had a real Irish taste for the bizarre—described what he calls a normal night at the Crow Street theatre:

The playhouse was then lighted with tallow candles, stuck into tin circles hanging from the middle of the stage which were now and then snuffed by a performer; and two soldiers with fixed bayonets always stood like statues on each side close to the boxes to keep the audience in order.

St Stephen's Green, Apollo room

The people in the boxes went in Court dress and behaved politely, but Trinity students were apt to break in and then the Quality went out fast, and the rest of the audience fell to battle. Many of the 'Bucks'—Tiger Roche and Buck English were examples—switched their shootings, riotings, woundings and thievings from Dublin to London and back. In London they were caught by the debtors' prison; in Ireland there was more licence because the authorities allowed them to let off steam in 'private' life, in order to keep it out of political action. In so far as the rioters were of immigrant stock, one can remark that, outside their own country, they were able to liberate the strong, suppressed theatrical capacities of the British.

The Bucks came up from the country to Dublin and some of their wildness has been put down to the fact of their military tradition: their fathers were Cromwellian soldiers who settled in their appropriated lands and spent the proceeds. The career of Buck Whaley has often been told; his family had collected a fortune and he spent it in wild gambling and eccentricities. The father came from Wicklow and was known as 'Burn-Chapel Whaley of Whaley Abbey, Ballinaclash'. He built the fine mansions at 85 and 86 Stephen's Green. The story is that the Buck, his son, jumped out of a window for a bet, to kiss the first pretty girl who passed in a carriage; this is untrue. But he did, they say, jump out of the drawing room window of Daly's Clubhouse in College Green on to a hackney coach. Others say the jump really occurred in Dover and that he was crippled for life. Dublin stories float about as light as air with the telling. The houses—now part of the University of Dublin—are more remarkable than the Buck. Here the *stuccadores* have created a charming scene of flowers, winged monsters, musical trophies and exquisite birds. 'Peacefully they feed their young or, rising with clamorous wing', writes C. P. Curran in his pamphlet *Norman House and University Church*, 'from the staircase walls they shriek stridently at the passer-by, they circle the ceilings in graceful flight or with beak and talon engage in death grapple with dragons.' It is thought that Robert West, a Dublin master builder, must have done this work. He had worked in stucco at the Rotunda Hospital and many great Dublin houses: he built and decorated 20 Dominick Street when Cramillion was finishing the fantastic ceiling at the Rotunda Chapel. West's family had been plasterers and builders since the early 17th century. Owing to the admirable labours of the Georgian Society, it has been shown that this beautiful stucco work was not exclusively the work of Italian

Stucco by Robert West, Dominick Street

and French masters; there was a notable number of Irish craftsmen. But Irish artists did 'abandon or fail to develop' figure decoration. The finest of the figures is Francini's Venus ceiling in the Bank of Ireland—the first introduction of the full-scale human figure to Irish stucco. At 85 St Stephen's Green the beautiful late Louis XIV Apollo panel is Francini's work.

The large number of native Irish, driven into Dublin by the Penal Laws and the misery caused by the land system, became the foundation of the terrible Dublin slums; but it would be hard to decide which was worse: Hogarth's London or the stinking Dublin of this time. Dublin *looked* worse, because it was much smaller, and because the lack of hope and the presence of degradation was, for the native Irish, national. Writing in 1965 of the general consequence of this, Sean O'Faolain says in his autobiography (and speaking of the early part of the present century) that the domination of an alien class

… even demanded the tribute of resignation and then sneered at us for the evasions and circumlocutions that have always been the last wretched self-destroying weapons of the poor and resigned the whole world over.

The nobility and gentry came up from the country to Dublin; the number of earls and viscounts was large; and there were the absentees, most of them with English estates and who did not like the hostilities and loneliness of Irish life, who nevertheless came over for a few months of the year.

All the memoir writers show that Dublin lived in a mixed state of reckless and rowdy bliss and of naked misery. The spendthrift landlords laid out their rents in enormous dinners; gambling was the passion. An enormous quantity of good claret was drunk—Dublin claret is still good—and the poor drank millions of gallons of spirits. At one time 2,000 ale houses, 300 taverns and 1,200 brandy shops were counted. About 1740 the mass addiction to whiskey came in. The slums stank, for there were no sewers; aggressive beggars attacked people outside their shops and houses. Certainly charity did something for the wretched and, particularly towards the end of the century, was a little more practical— there were said to be more charitable institutions in Dublin than in London. There was a need for the practical. There were epidemics of fever. The phrase 'Liffey fever' can still be heard; years ago I came across an old bookseller on the quays who said he had had it; it was of this fever that poor Molly Malone died.

But a shadow appeared in the sky of the 18th century. The great aristocratic

The Earl of Wicklow

57

period of improvers, planners and taste, was beginning to run out. Dublin was Europe's, and particularly England's, last aristocratic folly. In 1775 the American War of Independence began and—in a phrase always disagreeable to Englishmen and never, even today, really forgiven—'England's danger was Ireland's opportunity'; for England's only interest in Ireland from the beginning was not desire for Ireland but fear of the two earlier empires, the Spanish and the French, fear of Ireland being used as a base and forcing the encircled British to fight on two fronts. The two revolutions and the Napoleonic wars in the next thirty years were to change the status of Dublin totally.

Despite the severe restrictions obtained by jealous English manufacturers between 1663 and 1690, Ireland had prospered as an exporter, largely through Dublin, of butter, beef, hides and tallow. Now the situation was changed. The trade with America—and with America's ally, France—was lost. British troops were withdrawn and there was a real danger of a French invasion. The Irish or, to be exact, the Anglo-Irish and Scottish-Irish colonists in the North, feared for their power and their property and were determined to defend themselves; and patriotically and politically, for they resented being treated as foreigners or second-class citizens by the British. Now there was a chance for large helpings of independence from London. In the richer North of Ireland, from which angered Presbyterians were emigrating—among them, incidentally, the ancestors of Henry James—the ideals of the American revolution were strong and republicanism became a force. The famous Volunteers were formed, gaudy in uniform, well armed and rather much given to parades and demonstrations. The British, in their trouble, saw the light. Ireland and the Volunteers got Grattan's Parliament; the law prohibiting the export of wool was repealed. Free Trade with Great Britain was established and Dublin began to export its famous porter for the first time, Guinness and the other breweries having been established in the mid-century, to counteract the excessive drinking of spirits. The Penal Laws—which had been very much ignored for a generation or more—were to be repealed. (They were not, however: dirty play among powerful or quixotic factions on either side, as usual, prevented it; and the King was mad.) Still, Burke eloquently compared the Irish liberation to the 'glorious English revolution' of 1688. Grattan becomes Dublin's hero and orator. He passed through the ranks of the Volunteers drawn up outside the Irish Parliament House and declared in 1782:

Ranger, St Stephen's Green

I found Ireland on her knees. I watched over her with a paternal solicitude; I have traced her progress from injuries to arms, and from arms to liberty. Spirit of Swift, spirit of Molyneux, your genius has prevailed! Ireland is now a nation.

For Dublin, the years between the American War, the French Revolution and the Napoleonic wars, were rhapsodic, farcical, macabre, corrupt and finally disastrous.

The Volunteers, of course, split. Only their splendid uniforms united them. And it was they who endangered the freedom of the Irish Parliament in College Green. It was as corrupt as the London Parliament, though the Irish Parliament outdid its parent in oratory, even with Trinity's Burke in the English house. Both nations had to deal with their reactionaries. Of one, Grattan was to say he stood with 'a metaphor in his mouth and a bribe in his pocket, a champion against the rights of America, the only hope of Ireland and the only refuge of the liberties of mankind'. Wolfe Tone (also of Trinity), one of Ireland's few Europeans and real revolutionaries, said the Irish Parliament 'doubled the value of every borough monger in the Kingdom'. The rate paid by the British for a vote against the Colonies in the New Irish Parliament was 2,000 guineas plus a pension or a salary.

But the Volunteers were picturesque and if they became a preposterous political threat they produced farce in the person of the eccentric Earl of Bristol. The previous Earl, his brother, had made him an Irish Bishop, and later the Bishop became a Viceroy, a transfiguration that would have delighted the author of *La Chartreuse de Parme*. Some people, as sensitive, or perhaps as unworldly, as Jeremy Bentham and John Wesley, found him liberal and intelligent and even judicious; others 'a dishonest madman, a worse husband, licentious and blasphemous'. On the eve of the National Convention in Dublin, the Bishop-Earl was determined to be President and Dictator of the Volunteers. He cheerfully exclaimed, 'We shall have blood, my lord. We shall have blood'. His entry into the city had been fantastic for Dublin has a talent for crowd scenes: the pavements were lined with armed Volunteers, the windows were packed with spectators. The streets were 'ablaze with scarlet and green and gold and azure'. Grenadiers carrying Irish battle axes, delegates in green scarves streamed to the Rotunda, followed by artillery, the guns dressed out in ribands, each with a scroll on its muzzle, carrying the splendid if unusual phrase: 'Open thou our mouths, O Lord, and our lips shall show forth thy Praise.'

Cook Street

As he drove through the cheering crowds, the Bishop was dressed in purple with white gloves, gold fringed and gold tassels hanging from them, and buckles of diamonds on knees and shoes. He was surrounded by the gorgeous liveries of mounted servants. The great demonstration failed. The Bishop was not elected. J. R. Fisher in *The End of the Irish Parliament* writes: 'At a critical moment when the Catholic claims were being pressed hard by the Bishop and his friends [Sir Boyle Roche] rose and declared that he was commissioned by Lord Kenmare, the head of the Catholic Party, to say that the Catholics did not ask for any such change at present'.

Later on, Sir Boyle Roche admitted that this was a lie; the famous clown who is supposed to have smelled a rat, to have seen it floating in the air and to have nipped it in the bud, concealed under his taste for erratic metaphor a deadly political determination. The Bishop, despite his absurdity, comes off better; no doubt he was really a Stendhalian bishop at heart for he grew suddenly bored and went off to Italy, his spiritual home.

In fact the Volunteers had turned into Protestant extremists, and had missed the revolutionary tide. One could rely on any party in Dublin to be instinctively hostile to the Enlightenment, liberalism or any of its later derivations. What killed the Volunteers was the end of the American War and the presence of a large army of trained British troops in the country. No musical comedy troupe had a chance against them.

The real crisis for Dublin and for Ireland came with the French Revolution, the English war with France and the rise of the United Irishmen and the figure of Wolfe Tone. Here, once more, England was in difficulties and indeed fighting for her life—as she was to do in 1914 and 1940—and if bad weather had not scattered the French invasion fleet, and if the French admiral had not hesitated, Ireland would have been successfully occupied. The United Irishmen had become a military body under Wolfe Tone whose hatred of England was intense. He sought the destruction of the Anglo-Irish landlords, and although his followers were certainly not carried away, as he was, by the ideas of the French Revolution, they had their deep resentments concerning rents and tithes and they uttered for the first time the word Republic. By one of the ironies of Irish history the word came south from the manufacturing Protestant north. It was a word of horror to the Irish bishops: to them it meant Jacobinism, as it did to Burke and the majority of Englishmen.

Right
Our Lady's Home

Next two pages
Christchurch from the Waterworks

Whatever may have been felt by the insurrectionists in Cork and the country-side generally, Dublin was determined to defend itself against invasion. There was great alarm. Tom Moore wrote about the suspense in his *Autobiography*.

I will remember (well) in the night the rebels were to have attacked Dublin the feelings of awe produced through the city by the going out of the lamps one after another towards midnight.

But comedy, as usual, preceded the tragedy. Corps of yeomanry were formed and Barrington, in his Münchhausen-like collection of anecdotes and musings which have been a godsend to historians of this time, describes the antics of a corps of elderly gentlemen who lived in Merrion Square. On fine nights they wandered about, called on each other for tea and cards; on damp nights they patrolled in sedan chairs with their muskets sticking out of the windows.

The invasion and the rebellion failed and it left behind it horrible memories of massacre by troops, Protestants and Catholics, and revived fanaticism. The cruelties practised by both Irish and English are ghastly. Only a Goya could have faced the sight or thought of what happened in the countryside. The English (awakened by the urgent necessities of the Napoleonic war), the Anglo-Irish (in their fear for their dominant situation in Ireland) and the Roman Catholic hierarchy, opted for Union with Britain. It is true that by no means all Anglo-Irishmen agreed on this. The manufacturing interests were against it. It has been said also that the Castle—that home of *agents provocateurs*—encouraged the Rising secretly. A large number of the members of the Irish House of Commons delayed and delayed, so putting up the price of the bribes by which they were eventually persuaded to sell their votes. Well might the Dublin news vendors shout their cry of those days: 'Bloody news: last night's packet: bloody news.' The Anglo-Irish had given in.

And so the Irish Parliament voted itself out of existence. A British regiment was posted outside the Parliament House and no public demonstration was allowed. And so also an age voted itself into extinction—an age squalid in politics, but socially one of the cleverest and most amusing worlds (Barrington said) that Europe could offer. A word must be said for Barrington who was against the Union but whose financial activities have raised the eyebrows of historians. He is one of a long line of Irish gossips and masters of the tall story who recalls the Spanish type in Seville or Madrid, who are collectors of *cosas de*

Sacristan

España which only the *cosas* of Ireland can match. The difference is that most of the *cosas de España* are true, whereas in Ireland truth is the point of departure. This is not to say that all of Barrington is untruthful: his record of the famous bulls of Sir Boyle Roche in the Irish Parliament is authentic. This master of romping hyperbole drew his talent possibly from the collision of metaphors inherited from a mixed culture. Of the threatened French invasion he said: 'Here perhaps, sir, the murderous Marshall—law—men (Marseillais) would break in, cut us to mince meat, and throw our bleeding heads upon that table to stare us in the face!' And he made a pretty defence of the Union in these words: 'Sir, there is no Levitical degrees between nations, and on this occasion, I can see neither sin nor shame in marrying our own sister.'

Wolfe Tone stands out as the most spirited, romantic and attractive figure of these years, as Robert Emmet was to do a few years later. He was not the flashy figure which artists later portrayed. Barrington said 'his person was unfavourable, his countenance thin and sallow and he had in his speech a harsh guttural pronunciation of the letter "R"'. But everything about Tone's character charms and excites admiration: he was imprudent, visionary, frank, wild, courageous and witty. He captivated most of his enemies. We know him better than most of the Irish revolutionaries because, just before 'embarking on a business'— as he put it—with the French in 1796, he sat down in Paris to write his life in order to pass away the boredom of waiting and waiting for the French to make their minds up; and, with some premonition, to give his family a record. His father was a coachmaker and his brothers and sister were all adventurous. He tells of how when he was a schoolboy he used to go to Phoenix Park to the military parades and field days and reviews which have always appealed to the Dublin taste for soldierly displays.

Being this time approaching seventeen years of age it will not be thought incredible that *woman* began to appear lovely in my eyes and I very wisely imagined that a red coat and cockade, with a pair of gold epaulets, would aid me considerably in my approaches to the object of my adoration.

Against his will he was sent to Trinity to be made into a lawyer, but he hated that 'illiberal profession' and the hankering for the military life remained. He soon fell in love with a young girl, the grand-daughter of a clergyman, living in Grafton Street, and cleverly got himself into the family, for he was a good talker and musician. He was a penniless student and he eloped with her. Their marriage was delightful, though the pair were often separated. His longing for military life was strong enough to make him try to get into the British Army to fight against the American colonists. The war ended and so that chance failed. He went to London and then returned to Dublin, a lawyer, wrote a satirical novel and some pamphlets. At Trinity he had often amused himself by crossing the street to the Parliament House to hear what 'the geese were saying under the Goose Pie'—but these were tame geese, not the wild ones.

Tone was soon at the head of the United Irishmen and travelling about Ireland trying to get Protestants and Catholics together and arguing with recalcitrant priests. His notes on these journeys give an account of Irish life which is both indefatigable and comical. His good humour shows the outspoken Irishman at his best.

Arrive late at Ballinasloe, and get beds with great difficulty. Meet Mr Larking, the parish priest; a sad vulgar booby, but very civil to the best of his knowledge. * Mr Hutton falls asleep in company; victuals bad; wine poisonous; bed execrable; generally badly off; falls asleep in spite of ten thousand noises; wish the gentleman over my head would leave off the bagpipes and the gentlemen in the next room would leave off singing

(a wish that often arises in the head of the contemporary traveller in Dublin)

and the two gentlemen who are in bed together in the closet would leave off snoring: sad, sad! All quiet at last and be hanged!

He went to America to get foreign help for the rising and then to France and got promises from Carnot and met Napoleon who was silent. Paris delighted him at first but soon the delays drove him nearly mad. He dined too well, he went constantly to the theatre; he returned to his room with a thick head to write memoranda. In despair his humour always saves him and one can see how his talk must have charmed everybody for he talked as well to his Journal.

Tone was made for action:

Today is my birthday—I am 33 years old. At that age Alexander had conquered the world; and at that age Wolfe had completed his reputation and expired in the arms of victory. I have as good disposition for glory as either of them; but I labour under two small obstacles at least … want of talent and want of opportunities … I will endeavour to keep myself as pure as I can, as to the means; as to the end, it is sacred—the liberty and independence of my country first, the establishment of my wife and our darling babies next.

*Wolfe used pseudonyms in his memoranda: the Mr Hutton who fell asleep was himself.

But the delays continued and also there is a hint of that humiliation which attends the lives of agents, in the humorous remark that he is like the Turkish spy 'who passed forty years at Paris without being known or suspected'.

The account of the fatal expedition to Bantry is one of the best pieces of writing in Anglo-Irish literature. But for a gale as disastrous to the French fleet as the wreck of the Armada, the landing might have succeeded. England was lucky again. He well knew he might be hanged as a traitor if he was captured.

The wind continues right ahead so that it is absolutely impossible to work up to the landing place, and God knows when it will change. The same wind is exactly favourable to bring the English upon us... if we are taken, my fate will not be a mild one: the best I can expect is to be shot as an *émigré rentré* unless I have the good fortune to be killed in action; for most assuredly if the enemy will have us, he must fight for us. Perhaps I may be reserved for a trial, for the sake of striking terror into others, in which case I shall be hanged as a traitor and embowelled etc. As to the embowelling 'je m'en fiche'; if ever they hang me, they are welcome to embowel if they please.

In fact he was captured and cut his throat rather than be hanged by the British. He has no statue in Dublin.

If the hero of the time was Wolfe Tone, the villain of the Union was Edward Fitzgibbon, Earl of Clare who was determined to dish Pitt's policy of Catholic emancipation. The Dublin mob hated him. A few years before he had obtained the withdrawal of Lord Fitzwilliam, a popular, liberal viceroy; the Dublin crowd rioted and went to Fitzgibbon's house in Ely Place, with rope to hang him. Two good things can be said for Fitzgibbon: Dublin owed the Wide Road Commission to him and the Custom House.

When he died, the mob pelted his coffin with dead cats.

After the Union Dublin lost a hundred or more peers. The new ones, who had been bribed by titles, soon left. The lure of fashion and politics was London. The lawyers spryly took their place. Dublin had always been a paradise for them, for Irish life was consumed by property disputes; and absentees left lawyers to supervise their estates. With the doctors, the lawyers became the new aristocracy. There were 650 barristers and 1,500 attorneys in the city: 'one man in a hundred of the total population was a lawyer'. The doctors moved into the best squares. The Four Courts took the place of Parliament as the centre of Dublin life. Irish lawyers seem to have lived in a firework display of wit; and Irish wit has the benefit of a rich tradition of political and religious innuendo: the duels between the hanging judge, Lord Norbury, and the famous Curran, who defended the United Irishmen, get their bite from the general air of treachery in the country. At his trial for treason, in his famous speech from the dock, Emmet had addressed Norbury with the words 'My lord, were it possible to collect all the blood that you have shed into a common reservoir—for great indeed it must be—your lordship might swim therein'. When an ass brayed in the middle of one of his speeches in Court, Norbury said, 'One at a time, Mr Curran'. When we have stopped laughing we have to remember that Curran was fighting for the life of a United Irishman, and that Curran's own assistant was an informer paid by the Castle to spy on him! (The spy wrote *Sweet Lass of Richmond Hill*.) One has to appreciate in Dublin the conflicts of talent and admire the shameless and even deadly piquancies of heartless comedy. At a bar dinner when someone complained of the mutton in the presence of the same judge, Curran got his own back: 'You try it', he said, 'when it will be surely well hung.'

The rounding up of the United Irishmen and later of Robert Emmet's supporters is one of the horrible and disgraceful episodes in the history of the English oppression of Ireland. To the natural bloodiness of defeat in bloody times—and we have to remember the Jacobin Terror, in France—were added the corruption and treachery of informers, those shifty figures who appear continuously in the Irish struggle. When we pass that Church of St Catherine in Thomas Street outside which young Emmet was hanged, we shudder at the thought of the event: the betrayed young man standing on the gallows plank with the sack over his head, the silent terrorised crowd of thousands in the street. His young wife waves a handkerchief and faints. (Later she went mad and was always unstable in mind.) The plank is kicked away by the hangman who eventually slices off the head of the dead man with a butcher's knife, while the dogs rush to lick up the blood on the streets, and women dip their handkerchiefs in it, whether out of patriotism or from some instinct of primitive magic we cannot tell. The famous and chilling words of *The Wearing o' the Green* come back to one with a savage meaning: public hanging was a contemporary European orgy. In Ireland it was a commonplace of politics. At Arbour Hill there was a spot where the bodies of hundreds of United Irishmen were thrown: it was known as 'the Croppies' hole'.

VI

The Union was good for Dublin's trade as a whole, but bad for those industries which could not compete with the methods and capital of industrial England. From generation to generation now, the cry goes up for capital—especially for English capital. The pre-Union aristocracy had been good customers of the Dublin interior decorators, cabinet makers and furnishers. Before the Union, it was said by one bank, the peers spent £600,000 a year in Dublin and the members of the Irish House of Commons between two and three thousand a year. The loss was serious and the shopkeepers tried to make it up by extortion. The fact is that Dublin followed the colonial fashion; in colonies ordinary plain living is cheap, but imported 'luxury' goods are always dear. New York was equally extortionate in the same period. There was also another influence on the Irish economy. In the 18th century people believed in Fortune rather than in investment, showiness among those who could afford it and even among those who could not. We have only to look at the careers of the Anglo-Indian nabobs.

Dublin became stagnant in the 19th century. The political battle—and its emoluments—moved to London. Dublin became a middle-class city and, soon, Victorian in style, no longer fashionable, adrift in time. Architecturally this was no bad thing for the Georgian manner lasted until 1860, and the early Victorian manner that replaced it is graceful. The windows are wider than the Georgian but follow the demure and vertical idiom. Wellington Road with its immense width, its long lawns and lovely gardens, indeed a large part of the once well-off Pembroke Estate between the Canal and Ballsbridge, are dignified examples of Victorian domestic refinement. These purlieus were untroubled by the violence of the industrial revolution. The more modest quarters of Rathmines—the often satirised area of middling gentility and Dublin Pooterism, with an accent all its own—are a pleasure to walk in. And there are some remarkable Ruskinian buildings: the already mentioned Museum in Trinity, the Kildare Street Club. There are some fine churches—the fortress-like St Andrew's, the dramatic so-called Black Church, St Mary's Chapel of Ease, built of black Dublin calp by John Temper. It stands like some vampire on its hill looking down to Parnell

The Black Church

66

Square. It scared children in the neighbourhood at the end of the century, according to Austin Clarke, the poet, who was born a few doors from it. Any child who ran round it three times in the dark would meet the Devil himself on the third round. Once some Protestant children took him into a service there and he was terrified because he made what he supposed was the frightful mistake of crossing himself. One of the girls squeezed his hand affectionately and so exorcised his terror of the Reformation. There is St George's at the end of Upper Rutland Street, with its lovely peal of Sunday bells. There are the solemn railway stations.

The growing provinciality of 19th-century Dublin had some charm but it was also depressing. Politically it had nothing to offer but failures: the Emmet Rising of 1803: Young Ireland and the romantic but incompetent rising of '48; the Fenians of 1867; Parnell—running through this often cruel history is the murderous theme of the land wars. The centre of agitation and drama is not Dublin, but the country. The Irish capital becomes a backwater. It ceases to be the second largest city in the British Isles. Yet in England this is the great century of the provincial cities: Manchester becomes the world's byword for the industrial class war, Leeds, Sheffield and Middlesbrough become rich, and Birmingham becomes known as the best-governed city in the world. Two great movements: industrialism and the fight of thinkers, writers, philanthropists, clergy, philosophers and artists against its evils, enrich the violent urban scene. The English novel derives its force from it. Dublin is lucky to have been outside this struggle; but unlucky to be outside a great formative experience which transformed not only England, but most of Western Europe; and which, towards the last part of the century, was felt in Spain and Russia itself. The violent injustices suffered in peasant Ireland belonged to an old way of life: new and flourishing conflicts replaced them; and the man of the Manchester slum or the Birmingham factory had been pulled into the struggle of the labour movement and socialism. It looked to him—as it was to look to James Connolly in 1916— as if Ireland was living in a dream and obstinately refusing to take part in the real national cause: the fight for social justice. Industrial workers all over the world had their own fight against landlordism.

Yet the lucky aspect of life in Dublin in the 19th century was its relative freedom from pressure on the person. Racial pressure was strong. Social pressure was small. The tyrannical worship of work was non-existent. In Dublin, idleness and leisure reigned at one end; and awful, feckless poverty at the other. There

Henrietta Street

was no aristocracy or large commercial class to weigh upon the professions; nor was competition forced upon them. The Dubliner was free to regard industrial civilisation with an ironical and uncommitted mind. The English-Irish dialogue became an exchange of sarcasms of which Shaw is full, especially as English nationalism became militaristic, and imperial. The soldiers were in power and Froude, in his *History of Ireland*, assisted them by making the whole nasty business blandly moral. The Irish and English were diverted by each other's accents which both parties found, for some rather infantile reason, so picturesque—that they wrote them phonetically. Shaw makes Hodson, the English servant, talk like this:

'You talk of evictions! You that cawnt be moved until you've ran up ighteen months rent. Oi once ran ap four weeks in Lembeth wen oi was aht of a job in winter. They took the door off its inges and the winder aht of its seshes on me, an gev maw wauf pnoomownia. Oi'm a widower nah.'

Dublin was able—polite Dublin at any rate—to regard Irish life rather snobbishly, as being socially purer and holier than life across the Irish Sea. The Dublin poor, when they emigrated to England, were mystified and shocked.

Dublin's luck lay in its misfortune and in the paradox that the Union united it to nothing. Whatever damage the Union did to Dublin civically, politically and socially, it turned intelligent and sensitive men and women to intellectual and imaginative interests. Gaelic Ireland had been destroyed: the Anglo-Irish who had ignored it now set about recovering it, especially in poetry, in ballads and legend. Out of this movement was to come the spiritual force that eventually made Irish freedom possible. From Mangan to Yeats, this is the real achievement of the 19th century. Anglo-Irish, they prepared the way for something that can, perhaps, be called Irish again: the more Victorian on the surface, the less Victorian underneath.

For the most part it was the Anglo-Irish genius that led the way as Swift, Berkeley, Sheridan, Congreve and Farquhar had before, and as Maria Edgeworth did. Antiquarianism—an English and German invention—led poets like Mangan and Ferguson to the Irish language and legends. One sees, dubiously, the signs of change in Moore's *Irish Melodies* which he drew from the native ballads when he returned for three years from England. The complaint was that he bowdlerised them; and until non-Victorian Gaelic scholars got to work on the originals, an

Right
In the Coombe

Next two pages
St Audeon's

emasculated and watery refinement was common in Anglo-Irish literature. Barrington is rather coarse but telling on this subject:

> I recollect Moore being one night at my house in Merrion Square, during the spring of his celebrity, touching the pianoforte, in his unique way, to 'Rosa' his favourite amatory sonnet; now throwing up his ecstatic eyes to heaven, as if to invoke refinement; then casting them softly, sideways, and breaking out his chromatics to elevate, as the ladies said, their souls above the world, but at the same moment convincing them that they were completely mortal.

But these sentiments are not stirred by the pure sadness of *At the Still Hour of Night*. The talent of Moore lacked Irish vigour and was precariously caught between the false and the genuine. His links are half with Ireland, half with the thin Romantic sentiment then in vogue. (When Sir Walter Scott visited Dublin he was treated like a king. Ladies curtsied when he rode down Grafton Street.)

The decisive event of Irish life in the 19th century (though it was not felt so disastrously in Dublin) was the tragedy of the famine from 1845 to 1849. All Europe suffered. England had its Hungry Forties; Ireland had starvation. The famine drove the peasantry out by the million and halved the population. All Ireland had been haunted; nostalgia for a lost past is the theme of its songs and poetry: farewells to the dead, the mourning for departed souls run through them; but now the scene becomes ruinous: the nostalgia is for living persons who have gone away.

There is a sinister preliminary to the famine. Why, after the 1780's, did the Irish population suddenly grow to eight or nine millions (if that figure is correct)? The population grew suddenly in England, too, and this growth may have been due to the anarchic change in the social order and the misery caused by the industrial revolution. In Ireland, the alien land system, with its lack of security of tenure and its evictions, had completely demoralised the Irish peasant: all travellers report with horror on what they saw. Early marriage was an act of despair. The only *work* available was propagation.

The full story of the terrible famine years is told in Miss Cecil Woodham Smith's *The Great Hunger 1845-9*. The effect on Dublin was to crowd the over-crowded slums. In England there was the Poor Law under which the wretched who lived in the cellars and courts of Liverpool at least did not starve; in Boston and New York also the Irish emigrant found himself driven to the cellars and the roads. His portrait appears many times in Mayhew's *London Labour and the London Poor*, and immediately one is struck by the innocence of these rural people

Weaver

in an industrial society. Generations of misery had left them without the energy to fight for themselves. (Misery does not create revolutionaries, as the Young Ireland movement discovered in 1848, when, easily crushed, they stood before the packed juries of the British courts in Dublin. The court scenes recall those we have since heard of, in the last few years, in the American Deep South.) Dublin relied on charity and British and American first of all. A soup kitchen was established outside the Royal Barracks which served over 8,000 people a day, a hundred at a time. They filed into a forty-foot hut and were served a brew invented by Soper, the French chef of the Reform Club. This unfortunate man had worked out the amount of vegetable soup that could keep a human being alive. The story of *Oliver Twist* is bad enough; the Dublin story is unspeakable, though poor Soper was a victim of his situation. Fashionable life went on its usual way in the city: the century did not understand how violent it was. Laisser-faire was a dreadful economic philosophy: the smiles of philanthropy served only to show the teeth of the bland doctrine.

One extraordinary thing did happen. In 1849 Queen Victoria visited the paralysed city where even the lawyers had no work and where commerce had almost stopped. Miss Woodham Smith quotes from the Dublin *Evening Mail* just before the Queen's visit:

> The greater number of good houses in Dame Street, Grafton Street and other principal thoroughfares are in a dirty and dilapidated condition, the windows broken, patched with brown paper, or here and there stuffed with an old hat, the shops closed, and the wooden shutters covered with auction bills, railway tables, quack advertisements and notices from the Poor Law Commissioners or the Insolvent Court.

The *Mail* was a Tory paper and sarcastically suggested that the houses should be temporarily filled with decently dressed people.

Dublin did clean itself up a bit. It put on a brilliant show. The Marquess of Kildare protested that money should not be spent on illuminations but on 'her Majesty's starving subjects', but no one listened to him. Illuminations, parades and banquets went on. And the crowds were enthusiastic. The Queen was gay, simple, charming and above all, unafraid, in her young days. She drove about with almost no escort and at a time when assassinations were frequent and only a year after the '48 Rising. Hundreds chased her in every vehicle they could find. She laughed with pleasure at it and everyone laughed back. The friendly spontaneous gaiety of the Dubliners delighted her, as one can see from her

Back garden

Letters. Some have called the meeting a love affair. Dubliners no doubt liked her as they like all pretty women: they also like informal manners—and indeed in the poorest slum room and cabin, as every traveller has known, the courtly ease is remarkable. It is an inheritance from a much older culture than our own, and perhaps springs, as it seems also to do in the Highlands of Scotland and the Welsh hills, from the classless pride of clan or tribal life. It is a way of life that has always enhanced the person. Dublin may have had political hopes of the Queen— someone did jump forward to her carriage and shout: 'Mighty Monarch, pardon Smith O'Brien' (the leader of the Young Ireland rising) in Phoenix Park—but they discreetly forgot them in the excitement of the party. She was praised for that most un-Irish virtue: 'early rising and habits of punctuality' which the male author of the phrase said was an example to the rest of her sex. At the first State occasion she appeared in green Irish poplin, embroidered with gold shamrocks. The next day the poplin was pink. The streets were crowded when she went out. She even rode in a jaunting car. The ride was at once celebrated in a Dublin popular song: '"Be me sowl," says she, "I like the joultin' of yer Irish jaunty car".'

Why did nothing come of the delightful spree? The Queen could not stop talking about it. Politics, as Miss Woodham Smith says.

The Queen returned to Ireland three times, in 1853, 1861 and 1900, but she was less accessible to the most accessible people in the world: 'And the Irish people, abandoned to laissez-faire and the operation of national causes, had learned the frantic detestation and distrust of everything and everyone English...'

If the Victorian age was dull in Dublin it was relieved by Occasions. The city has always liked to be out on the streets. It has always liked something big to happen. It likes the theatrical and even the tawdry; but, next to a huge funeral, what it likes is a personage: indeed, a funeral really represents the apotheosis of the Person who is suddenly a celebrity in the brief time of the journey to the cemetery. The passion for funerals exists also in Wales; in Ireland it approaches the Italian. Grief has never been repressed in Ireland; the attitude to death and grief is one of the few non-Puritan traits of the Irish people; in their religion, it is certainly their only non-Puritan trait. The funeral has the allure of a procession and Dublin's appetite for processions is constant. There are the good, bad or indifferent, the pathetic, the silly, the shabby and the grand. But one thing is

Antiquities

noticeable in all. There is always a light in the eye of the processional man or woman however he or she may shamble. There is a comic but also grand contrast between the man and his particular protest. He walks silently but as if he were shouting inside himself. And even those whom he passes and who may violently disagree with his cause or despise it, will be stirred. The derisive one would, for two pins, join the processions for the irresistible pleasure of it. If he holds back, it is not because of restraint: but because the Occasion is not great enough for him, at that moment.

After the funerals, the great Occasions of Dublin in the 19th century were the greetings of political leaders, especially after the release from jail—jail having been for so long the most honourable address a man might have. When Daniel O'Connell, the Liberator, came out of prison 200,000 people are said to have greeted him—if this heroic estimate is correct, it would mean nine-tenths of Dublin's population, which sounds unlikely. He was borne on a triumphal chariot that had been drawn up to the prison walls by six dappled greys which (says Sir James O'Connor),

danced with delight. And what a chariot. Marvel of improvisation. It was built in three tiers or platforms. The topmost tier had a throne, gorgeous and roomy, for the popular deity. Him brawny arms seized, and with care and delicacy of touch—for he was no mean weight—they hoisted him, with the aid of ladders, to his lofty perch, flanking him at that giddy height with his son Daniel Junior on one side and his chaplain on the other.

On the middle platform, in solitary grandeur, was placed a grey-beard harper to beguile the time by patriotic tunes. The stability of the structure was ensured by the presence on the lowest platform of a pyramid of the grandchildren of O'Connell, apparelled in green velvet tunics and caps with white plumes.

The cortège slowly and perilously rolled into the city. The demagogue could not have had a more triumphal progress. Yet—how often one seems to have noticed this in Irish life—after the Occasion, things go flat. O'Connell was to die three years later and he was given a funeral as solemn as the progress from jail had been gay: but neither counted politically for anything. O'Connell had won Catholic Emancipation; but the cause of the Repeal of the Union was dead.

From the sixties on to 1916 Dublin dawdled in the general peace of Europe. Victorian Dublin—it is hard for us to realise—was a military city. Pictures in the newspapers show the regiments marching, the cavalry charging and the soldiers

Gravediggers, Glasnevin

hanging about in the streets. This was the time when uniforms were pretty, when the military life still had its touch of opera. Thackeray had noted:

of the numberless amusements that take place in the Phaynex it is not very necessary to speak. Here you may behold garrison races, and reviews; Lord Lieutenants in brown great coats; aides de camp scampering about like mad in blue; fat colonels roaring 'Charge' to immense heavy dragoons; dark rifle men lining woods and firing; galloping cannoneers banging and blazing right and left. Here comes his Excellency the Commander in Chief with his huge feathers, and white hair, and hooked nose; and yonder sits his Excellency the Ambassador from the Republic of Topinambo in a glass coach, smoking a cigar.... They love great folk, these honest Emerald Islanders.... They go in long trains to a sham court—simpering in tights and bags with swords between their legs....

To him Dublin Castle life had 'a very high life below stairs look'. 'Oh that humbug of a Castle. It is the great sham of all the shams in Ireland.'

Thackeray had arrived at the height of the railway age directed in Dublin by the genius of Dargan. The railways did much to pull Ireland together and meant everything to Dublin. It was Dargan who created the Royal Dublin Society's answer, in 1853, to the London Exhibition of 1851. The Queen came over again to it. A newspaper editor let himself go: I take this from Elizabeth Bowen's amusing book on the Shelbourne Hotel. It is a quotation from the *Exposition Expositor and Advertiser*.

Now, while with trumpet and banner and the acclaims of congregated thousands, the pageantry of martial attire and the gorgeousness of civic robes, the gleam of the warrior's cuirass and the flash of his now idle falchion, mingling among the banners of the sons of peaceful toil, and science and learning—now while all this tide of human life surges and swells and pours along the halls which has risen as it were at the touch of the enchanter's wand, a profound emotion agitates the heart.

All this in glass and iron and timber; a collection of Oriental bubbles and very pretty from the pictures one has seen of it. The Exhibition building faintly recalls Brighton Pavilion.

The aim, the old, old aim was to get capital into Ireland; if the hopes of rhetoric were not attained, Dublin does seem to have got more comfortable. For one thing, many of the absentees repented because London was too expensive; and many of the gentry who could not afford a London Season turned to the Season at the Castle. The season lasted from January to March. In his novel, *Drama in Muslin*, George Moore opens in the Shelbourne drawing room and gives

Boots repaired

a half-Irish, half-French naturalistic view of the gay life. Daughters were brought up from the country in the hope of catching a British officer. Suburban Dublin—Killiney and Dalkey—was becoming a less expensive Bournemouth or Cheltenham. It was possible to be grand on a poor pension. The 'quality' ruled and Dublin's long period of subtle middle-class snobberies set in; they lasted well into the 20's of this century and still have their echoes.

The subject of Irish snobbery is as intricate as Irish history. At its most acceptable it is an aspect of racial pride. I have an Irish friend who, in a dispute about his lineage, declared that his family went back to the year 1600. He was referring (he malevolently said) to 1600 B.C. He was a direct descendant of Milesian kings. There are other strains of racial pride: descent from the old Irish chieftains—any member of the clan can claim that; Norman descent—in England a joke, in Ireland a militant matter. Such racial snobberies are a native delicacy—and they are always carried abroad if the Irishman emigrates. Kinship is the Irish substitute for the class systems which Western European and American societies have evolved. It is no good putting on airs in Ireland, for everyone is very subtly putting on airs. At the old Abbey Theatre, actresses like Maureen Delaney and Sarah Allgood were expert in catching the dramatic facial expressions of this trait, which has been a gift to Irish comedy: the comedies of Sheridan and Wilde purported to be about London, but were really about Dublin. Only Shaw, inordinately sensitive to the idea of being a 'gentleman', marked the difference between England and Irish snobbery: in England it was full-fleshed and vulgar, an aspect of a mongrel and expanding society, whereas in Ireland, society had contracted. In England, the man or woman of humble origin who rises in the world and who becomes a snob is blatantly pretentious. In Ireland he sails into his adventure like a born actor. He easily takes to the careless disdain of being 'grand' and the only criticism one could make of his performance is that it is pernickety and sometimes precious. Dublin spots this kind of thing very quickly.

The Anglo-Irish or gentry snobberies of Dublin have greatly changed. But where they have lasted it is because the middle class, in the English sense, has been small, and because after the Union, when the peers left, certain middle-class elements became proto-aristocrats, rarely egalitarian or democratic. So the Anglo-Irish despised socially the Catholic Irish they had crushed, but were themselves split into those who could afford to send their daughters for a Season

Right
Arran Quay

Next two pages
Foster Place

in London and those who had to be content with the Castle; between those who sent their sons to Oxford and Cambridge and those who had to be content with Trinity. There is or was the pursuit of the English accent, the analysis of degrees of brogue, the mild apartheid between districts. I have been handed a guide to the landed gentry of Ireland by a suburban householder who said to me darkly:

'This is a very rare book. If anyone you meet here says he is this or that you can check whether he's telling the truth.' The thought that he might not be is a preoccupation. It contains an historical passion that has become fossilised. One cannot call it warmly pretentious as it would be in England: in Ireland it is cold.

The one great Irish novel of the 19th century, *The Real Charlotte* by Somerville and Ross, is framed in this central concern. An important part of the plot is about the attempt of a noisy, beautiful, careless, common girl from Bray—a place distinctly lower middle class—to marry into the gentry. She is cruelly subjected to the social inquisition, with the full approval of the authors who, in fact, find her so socially undesirable that they are obliged to kill her off at the end of the book. Snobbery has replaced sex as a natural force. Having established this freezing ethos, the authors are able to write a powerful novel about violent jealousy and corruption and one that can be compared, except for scale, with *La Cousine Bette*. It is a tale of the diverted passions of a small, defensive and decaying society, and it contains a masterly portrait of the lifeless, sexless, hopelessly neutral young upper-class man of the period. After the Treaty of 1922, when a large number of these colonials left Ireland for England they turned naturally to suburban England, at the same time (like returned Anglo-Indians) feeling able to despise it. If we compare them with the characters of Mrs Gaskell's *Wives and Daughters* or the people of *Pride and Prejudice*, we see they embody the angers and dullness of isolation, whereas the English novelists' characters have their place in a well-found if nowadays unacceptable social hierarchy.

In *The Real Charlotte* we seem to be looking at the other side of that notorious character, 'the stage-Irishman', who became established as a national figure in the Victorian age. His predecessors were the wild eccentrics like Buck Whaley and Tiger Roche who were really English types enlarged for the wilder Irish scene; Somerville and Ross and Lever are said to have invented him and used to be attacked for doing so by the solemn writers of the Gaelic Revival, and the puritanic supporters of Sinn Fein. The fact is that 'holy Ireland' inevitably produces an unholy counterpart. The stage-Irishman was not an Anglo-Irish

Master of the High Court

75

invention. He abounded. He still abounds. He is not necessarily an English hybrid: even when he is, this does not make him less real: Shakespeare's Fluellen can be found any day in Wales. The stage-Irishman can be found in all the Irish racial or religious groups. He exists as a peasant in Synge's *Playboy of the Western World*, as well as in the person of Flurry Knox: in Joxer Daly as well as in Sir Murtagh Rackrent: in *Finnegan's Wake* and most recently in that broth of a boy, Brendan Behan. The stage-Irishman is an exhausting professional but a little of him is a pleasure. Augustus John enjoyed a little of Gogarty about whose 'bounce' a Dublin ballad was written, but after a while was driven to throw a dish of peanuts in his face to shut him up. The stage-Irishman is born of Irish sociability. It is his particular vanity that he thinks he is 'having on' the stranger, and especially the English stranger; in this he is usually self-deceived.

On the whole, Dublin was getting more solemn towards the end of the century and certainly has gone through a prolonged solemn phase since 1922. But there are plenty of people who became professionally Irish. My last was a young one, already advanced on this well-known course, in Vancouver. As the train drew out and passed the grain elevators by the harbour he joined me in the bar.

'They've built those elevators quickly', he said.

'Are they new?'

'Sure the old ones were burned down two years ago. I set fire to them myself.'

'Go on!'

'Anyway they accused me of it. I backed a truck into the cable.'

'Were you hurt?'

'Not at all.' (Scornfully but the gentle voice was delighted.) 'There was a powerful explosion. They were burned to a cinder.'

He was entranced by a vision of some transcendental piece of destruction. The dialogue was the opening scene of one of the well-known, entirely foreseeable Irish acts. It relieved for a few moments the boredom of life: but a few moments are enough and one begins to plan one's get-away.

Out of the professional classes who ruled and diverted Dublin life in the 19th century came strong personalities. None can be called typical, because each was himself. In Trinity there was Mahaffy, a man of such virtuosity that, like an actor, he exists for us now only by hearsay and anecdote. He was not only a learned man: he was a first-rate cricketer and shot, wrote a book on fly-fishing and knew the pedigree, it is said, of every racehorse in Ulster. He adored royalty, who invited him to stay simply to hear him talk. Asked to define an Irish bull he replied: 'An Irish bull is always pregnant.' When he was told that one of his enemies was ill, he snapped 'Nothing trivial I hope'. Some of his *mots* have been cheerfully stolen so that lines like: 'In Ireland the inevitable never happens but the unexpected often occurs' or: 'An Irish atheist is one who wishes to God he could believe in God', have become part of the general Irish gag book and are now over-valued. Indeed Oscar Wilde, his pupil, can be said to have reorganised and perfected the art of his master. Mahaffy was one of the princes of the exquisitely insincere and fantastic school of Irish conversation, the kind which sails off into inspired saturnalia and which can never be remembered. People have said that Mahaffy was destroyed by his own versatility. It was an intoxication: word drunkenness, as *Finnegan's Wake* and, later on, Beckett have shown, is a consequence of mixing two powerful drinks: fantasy and pedantry. Apart, their effect is thin and feeble: mixed they are an irresistible addiction.

Another slightly earlier kind of personality of the lethargic period was Dr Wilde, the father of the dramatist. He takes one deeply into Dublin life. He appears in the non-political period that follows the failure of the Young Ireland movement. (Wilde was eventually to marry a patriotic poetess attached to the *Nation,* the famous Young Ireland paper: Dublin doctors often have close contacts with literary society.) Wilde was an energetic young man who had studied eye and ear surgery in London and Vienna, and returned to set up a clinic at the back of Molesworth Street for the free treatment of the poor. The place of public charity in Dublin is important: it is one of the 18th-century inheritances; privately the Irish are immediately charitable to all forms of failure and to all sins, except the sexual. Wilde's clinic was a huge success, for it was publicised in the way that Dublin prefers, and he was soon flooded with rich patients. He and his wife moved to Merrion Square and lived a Bohemian life. The long-drawn drama of his career there—strangely pre-figuring the tragedy that destroyed his son— can be read in Patrick Byrne's *The Wildes of Merrion Square.* For the brilliant doctor was energetically promiscuous and gregarious. The couple gave boisterous parties. These gatherings were famous. Mrs Wilde

... was a majestic figure, sitting in the twilight of her shaded lights. She adapted the Irish *brat* or cloak to modern use and adorned it with embroideries of ancient Celtic design.

Eventually Wilde became quarrelsome with friends, patients and students, took to hard drinking, neglected his person. 'Why', said Dublin malice, 'Why are Dr Wilde's nails always black? Because he scratches himself.'

In Wilde, we have the attractive and familiar spectacle of Irish versatility. He was not only a famous doctor, he had written travel books, a text book on surgery, edited a medical journal and was a serious archaeologist and antiquarian. He was surgeon-oculist to the Queen. He got a knighthood. Alas, he was pursued by one of his mistresses who accused him of seducing her while she was drugged and who went to the length of publishing the accusation in a pamphlet and getting newsboys to sell it outside a hall where he was lecturing. It is a terrible story of persecution for she trapped him into a libel action, in which however she got only a farthing damages. The tale ends dreadfully. When the doctor lay dying a great many years later, the lady came every day to sit by him.

... swathed in black and heavily veiled she would enter silently and make her way upstairs. None interfered with her. There she would sit for hours, nearly the entire day, like a Buddha, without speaking, almost without moving. Through the thick veil the eyes rested unceasingly on the haggard features of the dying man, whose half glazed glance returned hers uncomprehendingly.

She waited there until he was dead and in his coffin. Then went off and was never seen again. Vengeance? Madness? Sadism? Love?

It is a tale that might have been written by Le Fanu, the master of the story of spiritual horror. He lived a few doors from Dr Wilde. And both Wilde's story and the work of Le Fanu seem to point to a preoccupation with some haunting hatred or loss which may be embodied in the ghost or revenant and which so often underlies the surface preoccupations of Irish life. It is present in Emily Brontë and Henry James, indeed the whole James family inherit their strange sense of vastation from their Irish ancestors. Vigilance—which is in fact the sense of vigil as a ritual—is one of Le Fanu's favourite words.

Le Fanu was the son of a Dean and had the brilliance of the Sheridan family. Craig relates that his mother was one of the spirited Irish rebel girls who turn up in every generation: she stole Edward Fitzgerald's dagger from the house of Mayor Swan who had helped in his arrest. (Fitzgerald died of wounds in the affray.) Craig thinks that the story of Mr Justice Harbottle can be attached to a house in Aungier Street in old Dublin: it is a profoundly Irish story for the idea of retribution haunts the city where every street reminds one of violent

revolt, assassination and execution. A coarse hanging judge—who could have been Lord Norbury or (in the English revolution) Lord Jeffreys—is tracked down by the ghost of the man he has unjustly hanged and is hanged in turn.

Le Fanu's imagination was fed by things that must have lain and still lie in the Dublin unconscious. His ghosts are not stage-ghosts. They do not go clumsily clanking about with their heads under their arms. They are guilts. They patter two-legged behind their victims in the streets; retribution adds up its account night after night: the secret doubt—in people obsessed with secrecy—scratches away with malignant patience in the guarded mind. It is we who are the ghosts. Those are *our* steps which follow us; it is *our* 'heavy body' we hear falling in the attic above. We haunt ourselves.

In architecture, Victorian Gothic was coming in: Pugin and Ashlin were clearing the site for the Augustinian Church in Thomas Street; Deane and Woodward were building the Museum at Trinity. The Catholic University was started in St Stephen's Green. The Horse Show always brought over the absentees: the Shelbourne filled with them and with the gentry from the country. Their estates were falling into the hands of middle-men. Somerville and Ross characters filled the fashionable parts: those women with wind-fiercened complexions, long heads, and box-like bodies, with their sprained ankles, strained shoulders and frightful high spirits, all conscious of their family connections: those shrewd, lazy, talkative men in tweeds that were hairier and pleasantly shabbier than the English variety. They had caught the native Irish feyness. They were easily angered, raging against the agrarian murders, the ruin caused by emigration. Scornful but envious of the English visitor, the gentlest among them talked of Biarritz and Rapallo; the sporting among them talked about the horse. It is not a freak of satire that, in the beginning of Anglo-Irish literature, Swift drew the Houyhnhnms as a master race. He had detected the national religion. In the next century Yeats would be seen in grey topper on the course; and more than one dead sportsman lay under a wreath done in his racing colours.

After 1860 the population of Dublin began to rise again to 300,000; something—if not much—was at last being done about the land. Parnell, regarded as a traitor by his own class, was succeeding against the British in the House of Commons in London. Despite Parnell's imprisonment in Kilmainham, despite the ghastly incident of the assassination of Lord Frederick Cavendish and Mr Burke—the head of the Castle—in Phoenix Park, despite even the downfall

Royal Dublin Society Horse Sales

of Parnell that split Catholic Dublin and created a feud that divided as bitterly as the Civil War was to do in 1923, Dublin and Ireland looked more contented than they had done for a century. Patrick Pearse indeed saw in this contentment something that must be broken. Disheartened by the Parnell affair, contemptuous of Irish provinciality, one of the cleverest students of the Jesuits and the Catholic University College, James Joyce left Dublin and his Church for Paris and spat at Irish politics. It has been said that disgusted by Tim Healy's part in the destruction of Parnell, he chose Ibsen as the new God. He might have said, as Yeats was to write much later on:

> Out of Ireland have we come.
> Great hatred, little room,
> Maimed us at the start.
> I carry from my mother's womb
> A fanatic heart.

He left Ireland when the Gaelic League and the powerful foundations of the Irish revival had been laid. Ironically, it is Joyce, the artist and exile who chose Europe and European culture, who portrayed Dublin for the first time in its history; and by the accident or intuition of art perceived the coming role of the city. Irish freedom would be attained not by invasions or country bands, not by the peasantry, but by the city itself and a new and hitherto voiceless element: the urban workers and lower middle class.

In the first twenty-five years of this century one can discern two distinct Dublin strains. There is the plain Anglo-Irish Dublin about to lose its ruling power just as the high bourgeoisie all over Europe would lose theirs. They have produced, as their opposite numbers did in Europe, a dissident class of brilliant thinkers, writers and artists—a movement which contains the names of Marx, Freud, Bergson, Proust, Yeats, Eliot, Forster, Lawrence, and which has not been surpassed in the post-1918 world. And there is vulgar Dublin, as drab, squalid and pathetic in its commonplace as any big city, but celebrated by Joyce down to its very shop signs and tram tickets, as no other city in the world has ever been. *Ulysses* is unforgettable because it has been written, as Joyce said, by its own people; they—and this is why Joyce is so close to them—are grammarians.

Dubliners, A Portrait of the Artist as a Young Man, Ulysses and *Finnegan's Wake* contain the mean, commonplace consciousness of the city in his day, in all its

James Joyce, death mask

pathos and desuetude, in the drama of its gossip, sins, indulgences and the twists and turns of rhetoric; his books drag us from street to street. One could use them as a guide to a past age. And also to the present one. For although Dublin has changed and no more Vestals will drop plum stones from the top of Nelson's Pillar at the feet of the 'one-handled adulterer' who meant so much to Dublin's sexual furtiveness, the new Dublin meditates as Bloom meditates. It is still a city fascinated by the money made by pubs.

Where do they get the money? Coming up red-headed curates from the county Leitrim, rising empties and the old man in the cellar. Then, lo and behold, they blossom out as Adam Findlaters or Dan Tallons. Then think of the competition. General thirst. Good puzzle would be crossing Dublin without passing a pub.

Of policemen and of endless street-corner stories:

I was just passing the time of day with old Troy of the D.M.P. at the corner of Arbour Hill there and be damned but a bloody sweep came along and he near drove his gear into my eye. I turned round to let him have the weight of my tongue when who should I see dodging along Stony Batter only Joe Hynes.
– Lo, Joe, says I. How are you blowing? Did you see that bloody chimney sweep near shove my eye out with his brush?
– Soot's luck, says Joe. Who's the old bollocks you were talking to?
– Old Troy, says I, was in the force. I'm in two minds not to give that fellow in charge for obstructing the thoroughfare with his brooms and ladders.
– What are you doing round these parts? says Joe.
– Devil a much, says I. There's a bloody big foxy thief beyond by the garrison church at the corner of Garrison Lane.

That is talk straight from the gutter.

The elements which make the works of Joyce the Dublin Bible are lasting in Dublin life. On the surface he is writing about the dirty, lice-ridden, flea-bitten, boozy and soldier-infested lower-middle-class city of the horse age which has almost gone. But the fundamentals have not changed. Once he had moved away from the naturalism of *Dubliners*, he did what all Dubliners do: he created a myth. Those words 'a bloody big foxy thief' are a simple instance of myth-making. He also extracted an essential by seeing Dublin in the terms of its habit of the 'talking mind': if ever consciousness could be described as a stream, that stream is Dublin's. The mind of Dublin is naturally dramatic: a great deal of ordinary Dublin can be put on the stage, just as it is, and it is no surprise that

Mulligan's bar

Ulysses and *Stephan D* have been used by the theatre. Only a little less important is the fact that Joyce has seized upon the familiarity of the city. The myth is not poetic; it is prosaic and familiar. Dubliners are plagued by a saturation in the place: it is not that it is 'the whole world' to them for Dubliners have never been in danger of losing the Irish race-consciousness, despite the intense intimacy of the relationship with England which has been the foundation of the city: if Dublin is not 'the whole world' it is 'a whole world': that is to say it is a place, as Joyce imagined in *Finnegan's Wake*, that might contain the slurred idiom of a weary myth of human life. Joyce's originality, his Dublinishness, lay in the anti-Gaelic, anti-heroic search for the mythical in the vulgar. It was natural for him to find his starting point for *Finnegan's Wake* in the old Dublin vaudeville song with its overtones of stage-Irishry and the wild Round-the-house-and-mind-the-dresser spirit of the jig. It has the whiskey, the neighbours, and a fight:

> *Then Peggy O'Connor took up the job,*
> *'Biddy' says she; 'you're wrong I'm sure'.*
> *But Biddy gave her a belt in the gob,*
> *And left her sprawling on the floor;*
> *Oh, then the war did soon enrage;*
> *'Twas woman to woman and man to man,*
> *Shillelagh law did all engage,*
> *And a row and a ruction soon began.*

A corpse who jumps from the bed—

> *Bedad he revives, see how he rises,*
> *And Timothy rising from the bed,*
> *Says 'Whirl your liquor round like blazes,*
> *Bad luck to your sowls—d'ye think I'm dead?'*

With a

> *Whack fol the dah, dance to your partner*
> *Welt the flure yer trotters shake.*

But notice, even in a vulgar ballad about the traditional subject, 'the revenant', and then see Joyce drag the history out of Dublin from the time of the Danes to the goings-on in the 'Fiendish Park' and that peculiar shrine of Dublin, the church called the 'Adam and Eve', still standing among the ruined quays:

And the strut of him! How he used to hold his head as high as a howeth, the famous eld duke alien, with a hump of granduer on him like a walking wiesel rat. And his derry's own drawl

Phoenix Park, Sunday

82

and his corksown blather and his doubling stutter and his gullaway swank. Ask Lictor Hackett or Lector Reade of Garda Growley or the Boy with the Billycub. How elster is he a called at all? Qu'appelle? Huges Caput Earlyfaulter. Or was he born or was he found? Urgothland, Tvistown on the Kattegat? New Hunshire, Concorn on the Merrimake? Who blocksmitt her saft anvil or yelled lep to her pail? Was her banns never loosened in Adam and Eve's or were him or her but captain spliced?

Dublin disappears into its own ancient, scatted mind. It is Joyce, rather than Yeats, AE and the great Anglo-Irish figures of the end of the century who, no doubt against his intention, points to the future; ruling Dublin will henceforth draw on popular philistinism.

We get a gentler and more intimate picture of modest Dublin life at the beginning of the century in Austin Clarke's *Twice Round the Black Church*. This church is close to Broadstone—the Galway station—and stands on its hill looking down upon the King's Inn. It is close to the beautiful Blue Coat School—and also on the way to Mountjoy Jail. The poet remembers seeing the Black Maria full of men and women prisoners laughing and shouting at the windows at the back of the van. There would be politicals among them. On Holy Thursday, it was the custom of Dublin women and children to visit seven churches. 'How many chapels have you done?' was the question. The choice was vast. Catholic Dublin has its chapels, its convents, its charities, its hostels and schools and missions in pretty well every street. The decorous and chattering young chapel pilgrims had a romantic, foreign-sounding choice of Carmelites, Discalced Carmelites, the Augustinians, Franciscans, Dominicans, Fathers of the Holy Ghost, Marists, Jesuits, Redemptorists, Vincentians. The custom has been done away with—I can't think why, for although religious observances in Dublin strike one as being conventional, there is an unmistakable look of eager anxiety on the faces of the faithful. I have seen men running anxiously, prayer book in hand, to mass, with an expression on their faces that one sees nowadays perhaps only on the faces of elderly Welsh Baptists. The habit of making the sign of the cross as you pass a church or convent is still common in Dublin—I have seen a young man in running shorts, practising for some race, pause to cross himself as he ran past Haddington Church; and bus conductors pause, as they hand you your ticket, to do the same if they catch sight of the cross out of the corner of their eye as the bus sways past. It requires an art to clip a ticket, take the money, cross yourself and keep your balance all at the same time. Taxi drivers, as in

Orphans

Spain, will take their hands off the wheel to do the same. And, ten years ago, on the journey on top of the Dunleary bus into Dublin, the passengers were continually crossing themselves. It is astonishing to see the members of the Dail or Senate at Opening Prayers make this gesture en masse. One sees that in no other Catholic country. At Westland Row Station, early in the morning, the male passengers pop quickly into the church next door for a few minutes on the way to the office. Is the Dubliner a very cautious man or woman? Is he constantly insuring himself? Or is it evidence of the dramatic, anxious inner nature of Puritan or Jansenist religion? I think the last.

VII

The official commemoration of the Easter Rising has just been held in Dublin as I write. The British have astonished Dubliners by regarding the men of the Rising as heroes; it would be easy to say about this admiration that it is one more example of the English habit of forgiving those you have injured. Certainly the English have short memories and the Irish have long ones: in fact the admiration has two more serious sources. First: in this year the British are remembering the loss of an equally patriotic and romantic generation, tens of thousands of them Irish, who lost their lives on the Somme. Secondly: the mass of British people in 1914 found it intolerable that an Irish settlement should have been delayed by a powerful section of their ruling class who were as oppressive to them as they were to the Irish. The Rising and the War disposed of those troubles.

Only one act of violence preceded this year's commemoration. Acts of violence are likely to last for ever in Ireland, for the Irish are privately vain of their taste for illegality and they enjoyed the gesture for its own sake. To commemorate the Rising, Kilmainham Jail, which had been in a state of ruin for years, was put into order and was opened as a sort of national shrine. In November 1965 I went to see how the work was getting on. Hundreds of tourists—mainly Irish-Americans—have visited the ruined jail every year. They scribble their names on the walls of the cells of this prison where so many Irish patriots were incarcerated, hanged or shot since the days of the United Irishmen. Here the leaders of the Rising were executed by the British. The jails of Ireland and especially of Dublin are old and brutal monuments. Kilmainham, in its rough granite, is the most horrible of them.

The driver who takes American tourists to visit the jail is eloquent about the brutality of British oppression; the British visitors are treated more guardedly. My driver, an old man who had fought against the British and who said his heart had been broken and his faith lost in the Civil War, was disgusted by my visit. The place, he said, was a monument to all the lies and betrayals of Irish history. He wanted the jail to be pulled down.

Inside, it was half-ruined. The roof had collapsed at one time, the grim little cells were rotted by damp, the floors had gone, one walked down freezing, dark, wrecked corridors, groping from plank to plank. One of the workmen, an old man who was doing some repairs, took me round the cells of the leaders of the Rising. We saw the broken gibbet on which (I believe he said) the Invincibles were hanged. He told the details of what each man had done. I saw the large cell which had two windows and which looked out on to a stone wall, where Parnell had been briefly imprisoned. His bust was there and there was an inscription cut into the sill. We went out into the exercise yard which is enclosed between the main block of the prison and the enormously high outer granite wall and then into the bleak yard where some of the men of the Rising were executed. In one corner was the spot where Connolly was shot. He had been badly wounded and carefully nursed in hospital—until he was well enough to sit up in a chair for execution! Nausea and hatred make the visitor wretched. The very fact that there are new granite chips in this death yard somehow appals. It is good for those of us who have escaped political imprisonment which, since 1916, has become a commonplace in our world, to consider the scene. Pearse longed to shed his blood: the British foolishly gratified his desire. From Tone and Emmet onwards the Irish patriot has always *wanted* to die. There is a most curious, obsessional desire in Ireland for 'the last rites', life having only a doubtful meaning.

And then, at the most wretched moment of my visit, the absurd occurred, as it does again and again in Ireland. I was just about to leave when another visitor got into the prison. He had found the door open and he wandered towards us, a well-dressed, cheerful, vigorous-looking man in, I suppose, his early sixties; he looked like a prosperous business-man. He was English.

'I hope you don't mind', he said. 'I was passing by. I thought I'd like to drop in on the old place. God, they've let it go. What a mess! What a shame! It wasn't like this in my time, the British kept it up, spick and span and proper. It's terrible. Oh yes, I was here. I was a naughty boy. They put me up there—in number three or four was it?—in the top gallery.'

The old workman had been wary but at this he woke up.

'What was it?' he said.

'Well', said the man, 'I've led a bit of a roving life, all over the world you might say, back and forth. I was a deserter. I was stationed in Galway. I was only a kid and I got into a spot of trouble down there—nothing really bad, well, we

Right
Kilmainham Jail, Parnell's Cell

Next two pages
Kilmainham Jail

won't go into it now, it's a long time ago. Nowadays they'd let it pass but those were hard times. That's where they put me, up there.'

'Is that a fact?' the old man began to grin.

'Yes, that's it, number three or four, top gallery. The man next door went mad and threw himself off and killed himself. There was no net in those days. What am I saying? I'm telling a lie. I was in here twice. That was when I was in Cork—more trouble, I deserted again. I deserted twice.'

'Did you now?' said the old man who had his hands in his pockets and was scratching his legs with delight.

'Let's see the exercise yard', the Englishman said. 'It's through there if I remember right.'

The old man said: 'That's right. Through this door.'

'Do you see that? He remembers it!' the old man whispered to me laughing. 'Come on now, I'll show you.'

'It's a shame the way they've let it go', said the Englishman.

'No one seemed to care at all about it', apologised the old man.

'Oh, here it is', said the Englishman, aglow to be in the yard. 'That's it. I reckon I know every stone in that wall. They made you run close to it. I have run round that wall hundreds of times.'

'You're right there', said the elated old man.

'And the drummer—now where did he stand? Over there by the window in the corner, I think', said the Englishman.

'In the corner it was. You see he remembers everything', the old man said with admiration.

'Left, right, left, right, pick 'em up. The drum tap!' said the Englishman.

'Ah, the drum tap! The drum tap, it made you skip', cried the old man.

'The drum tap! They knew how to beat it out fast.'

'Ah, they did that.'

Reluctantly the Englishman left his playground.

'Was it in the Devons or the Foresters you said you were?' asked the old man.

'The Foresters.'

'I was in the Fusiliers', said the old man. 'We were in the Curragh.'

They were charmed and they chattered. The Englishman gazed up at the cell.

Caretaker

'I think it was the third cell, perhaps I'm mixing it up with the second time. Or Arbour Hill Barracks—they had me there too. That was the third time.'

'Three times. Powerful', said the old man whispering. And then, covering his mouth with his hand, he giggled: 'I was in the bloody British Army too. I was a deserter myself. Ha! Ha!'

'Where were you then?' said the Englishman.

'I was in Solingen, never short of a razor blade there. And the girls cheering in the street when we got in', said the old man.

'You're bloody right. I was up there too!' said the Englishman. The two friends gazed at each other.

'It's a pity, it's a great pity it's been let go', the old man said.

'It's a shame. It looked decent once. To be candid I came here because I had a bit of trouble with my daughter. I'd forgotten all about it—well, the years go, you forget. But she found out and "Oh dear, our dad in prison!"—you know? She was so upset I had to get the priest to calm her down. It's all right now. So, I thought, next time I'm over I'll have a look at the old place. I didn't expect this mess.'

'Oh we're putting it right. We're getting in the show cases; there's been a delay in the cement', apologised the old man. 'But we've got the toilets nearly finished. We're waiting for the pipes. It's in the Commandant's office. I'll show you. We've done a nice job here.' We went into the toilets.

'That's it', said the Englishman. 'They brought you in here. That's where he must have sat.'

Toilets for tourists: is that how the history of a human agony ends?

EPILOGUE

The inevitable fanatics remain, but the quarrel is over. In the middle of the ballad-singing at Howth one of the performers will tell a comic story about a drunken Irishman who has a bantering chat with St Peter at the heavenly gates. Suddenly the joke turns serious: 'But give us back our Six Counties!' he cries out with passion to St Peter and the audience of gay young men and women applaud with united vehemence. Except for the question of Partition the quarrel is over. Or as near over as it ever will be. Dublin's relations with London are excellent. After a long spell of disheartenment, the city has become prosperous and the people hopeful though worried. They know that they are far behind the rest of the world in education and they wrangle about the cause of this: is it due to an old-fashioned priesthood, the confusion that has arisen because of the attempt to revive artificially the once lost Gaelic, to apartheid in the universities? About education Dublin is getting very angry. Dublin Bay is one of the most beguiling lagoons in the world, the roads of Ireland are empty: is it better to preserve the quiet paradise of an empty country? Don't all the visitors from the overcrowded industrial nations breathe with relief when they come to this blessed spot? Yes, say some of the thoughtful Dubliners, but isn't mediocrity the price? Aren't they held back by the old Irish fear of speaking out, the inborn deviousness? No (says Aarland Ussher), the Irish are not timid; they are proud and have a disbelieving disdain for communal life. Writers like Sean O'Faolain and Frank O'Connor have lashed out against the evil; and even more at the now successful middle class 'utterly devoid of moral courage'. The theatre, once important, is in a poor way. Actors and actresses leave Dublin for London. The Abbey has now one of the most up-to-date theatres in Europe, but there are no plays. Almost none of the brilliant new playwrights of Europe, America or Great Britain have been performed in Dublin. Ruling Dublin is still suffocated by an austere self-love and provincial chauvinism. We can be certain that the rows caused by *The Playboy* would occur again if foreign plays were brought in.

If Dublin is less exciting than it was forty years ago we can only say that revolutionary periods are followed by tedious years of adjustment and reconstruction and that the real achievements of Dublin have been in industry which had scarcely existed and—I am told by English academics—in science. But, with all the changes, this is still a place for simple pleasures. Time does not exist, night turns into day, cars stream by until the small hours; after midnight is the busiest time for taxis which are idle half the day. The pubs and sports grounds are packed, so are the dance halls. (The dance, with its easy ceremony, its formalisation of display, and its unsexed or sublimated philandering, and its protective gaiety, has always been a Dublin taste.) Cafés and restaurants are crowded, though not the two or three best restaurants where few Dubliners can afford to eat. Women begin to go to pubs, and in the last year or so the traditional barman or 'curate' is being replaced by pretty girls who raise the tone. The famous segregation of the sexes is said to be coming to an end: this change is still in the nervous stage. To a professional photographer, a woman, it is suggested with immense circumlocution and tact that it would 'look better' if she explained she did not earn her living in this way, but took photographs for pin money!

Ireland used to have the lowest marriage rate in Europe, and the age of marriage was very late; but there is now a small increase in the number of early marriages. This must be due to some loosening of the severe restraints of Irish life, though it still strikes one that Dublin is a male-dominated society and that the object of the male is never to go home. And especially always to be late for dinner. An Irish childhood must be one of the happiest in Europe for this is the country of high animal spirits; and the temper of childhood persists late into life.

'We're ready now, Captain', says the chef at Jammet's, putting his head into the bar. The Captain ignores this. He is in full monologue with a friend and reaches for another whiskey. Time passes.

The chef appears angrily.

'Come on now, Major. You have us destroyed in here.' Military promotion being a frequent recourse where drinkers are recalcitrant. As a boy the Captain certainly made it a point of male honour to come in late for meals and mother admired him for this manly trait. It gave her the chance to use her tongue. There is exceptional tolerance of drunkenness. It is often said that the sexes do not like each other and fear sexual life. The reason given for this is that, since the father is always out at the street corner, or the bar, or the sports ground, with

Right
Huband Bridge

Next two pages
Left: Eavan Boland
Right: The younger generation

90

his friends, the power of the woman in the home increases. The mother dominates her son, and his feelings are directed first to her and then to his sisters: this tends to make him idealise and—eventually—to despise women. Guilt about the mother is a recurring subject in Irish literature: the peculiar relationship existing in James Joyce's family and described in *Ulysses* is an example. One has the impression of Irish love being militant flirtation, a meeting of enemies who unite for a moment and then return chastely to their own separate ways of living. Under the command of the mother, the bonds of family life are far stronger than they are in England or America. The mother's desire is for a guard of obedient bachelor sons who can do what they like, but they must be trained to be wary of other women.

At lunch time Dawson Street is full of gay, chattering, pretty girls; in the evening, they cling together and are sad. Sociability and 'the gaiety' or a quarrel will stir their quick tongues and sociability is the alternative to emotional life. And there is the religious attitude directed by the priest through the mother. Gogarty, in one of his outbursts about the censorship which up to a few years ago was the most repressive in the world, has this sentence: 'It is high time the people of this country found some other way of loving God than by hating women.'

Dubliners are still shocked by the wickedness of England and go there for a holiday from virtue. The fact is that it is very much a city caught by anxieties, for it is half way between an old way of life and a new one. It is crowded with country people who bring with them the obduracy, the gossipy pleasures of small-town life. Shop assistants gather in corners excitedly whispering, and if an impatient customer calls to them, they turn with offended astonishment at him, wondering who 'the stranger' is as all country girls do, and then turn round and go on whispering. Shops, in the country, are meeting places. Before anything else Dublin is dedicated to gregariousness, to meeting people, to welcome, to the longing to hear who they are and what they will say. As you walk down St Stephen's Green past the Shelbourne or the clubs, indeed as you walk down any street, in the wealthy quarters or the poor, you see the man or woman who is coming towards you pause for a second. They gaze at you perplexedly, search your face, even smile to convey that they wished they knew you, and not knowing you, are puzzled by this break in the natural order. They ache for acquaintance; and if they don't find out who you are they will invent it. This instant

Two sisters

accueil is part of the charm of Dublin which glows with promises and with promises to mend broken promises, which sparkles with guesses, which loves to agree and reserves the private pleasure of not really agreeing at all. You are in fact walking among the preliminaries of a life-long duel.

Index

Index

Abbey Theatre, 13–15, 74
'Adam and Eve' Church, 82, 83
AE (George William Russell),
    5, 17, 18, 19
Alberti, Leon Battista, 53
Allgood, Sarah, 14, 74
Aras an Uachtaran (President's
    House), 33
Arbour Hill, 65
Arbour Hill Barracks, 11
Atha Cliath (Dublin), 43
Aungier Street, 78

Baggot Street, 21, 32
Baggot Street Bridge, 32
Ballinasloe, 63
Ballsbridge, 9
Bank of Ireland, 37, 57
Bantry, 64
Barrington, Sir Jonah, 55, 61–2, 69
Beckett, J.C., 45, 77
Behan, Brendan, 16, 76
Belfast, 27
Belvedere College, 42
Belvedere House, 54
Bentham, Jeremy, 59
Bergson, Henri, 80
Berkeley, Bishop George,
    25, 50, 51, 68
Binchy, Professor D.A., 43
Birkenhead, Lord, 5

Black Church, the (St Mary's Chapel
    of Ease), 66–7, 83
Blackrock, 23, 38
Blessington, Lady, 54
Blood, Colonel Thomas, 47
Bloom, Leopold, 42, 81
Blue Coat School, 51, 83
Boland's Mills, 9
'Botany Bay', 52
Bowen, Elizabeth, 73
Brazen Head, the (tavern), 47
Bridewell Police Station, 10
Bristol, Earl of, 59
Brontë, Emily, 78
Bullock Harbour, 38, 39
Burgh, Thomas, 52
Burke, Edmund, 49, 59, 60
Burke, Mr (head of Dublin Castle), 79
'Burn-Chapel Whaley
    of Whaley Abbey', 56
Butler family of Kilkenny;
    see Ormonde, Dukes of
Byrne, Patrick, 77

Carlyle, Thomas, 30
Casement, Roger, 8
Cashel, 43
Caulfield, Max, 10
Cavendish, Lord Frederick, 79
Chapel Royal (Dublin Castle), 37
Charlemont House, 51, 73

Charles I, King, 52
Chesterfield, Lord, 49, 50
Chesterton, G. K., 17
Christchurch Cathedral, 44
Clanmorris, Lord, 55
Clare, Edward Fitzgibbon, Earl of, 64
Clarke, Austin, 36, 67, 83
Cloncurry, Lord, 51
Clontarf, 43
Clough, Arthur Hugh, 30
College Green, 56, 59
Collins, Michael, 12
Congreve, William, 51, 68
Connolly, James, 7, 8, 9, 67, 86
Coombe, the, 48–9
Cormick, F. J., 14
Cosgrave, William T., 5–6
Craig, Maurice, 34, 37, 46, 48, 52, 78
Cromwell, Oliver, 48
Crow Street Theatre, 55–6
Crowe, Eileen, 14
Curran, C. P., 53, 56
Curran, John Philpot, 65
Curtis, Edward, 43
Custom House, 33, 36, 51

Dalkey, 23, 38, 74
Daly's Clubhouse, 56
Dame Street, 70
Dargan, James, 73
Davis, Thomas, 25–6, 34, 53
Dawson Street, 91
Deane, Thomas, 79
Delaney, Maureen, 14, 74
Delany, Mrs Mary, 54

Dickens, Charles, 29–30
Dillon, Myles, 43
Djouce, 24
Dominick Street, 56
Dorset Street, 37
Dublin Bay, 23, 43, 89
Dublin Castle, 37, 45, 73
Dublin Mountains, 6
Dublin University, 42, 56, 79, 80;
    see also Belvedere College;
    Trinity College
Dunleary, 7, 19

Edgeworth, Maria, 68
Eglinton, John, 13
Elgin, Lord, 35
Eliot, T. S., 80
Elizabeth I, Queen, 52
Emmet, Robert, 34, 53, 62, 65, 67
English, Buck, 56

Farquhar, George, 51, 68
Ferguson, Sir Samuel, 68
Fisher, J. R., 60
Fitzgerald, Barry, 14
Fitzgerald, Edward, 78
Fitzgibbon, Edward; see Clare, Earl of
Fitzwilliam, Lord, 64
Fitzwilliam Square, 37
Forster, E. M., 80
Four Courts, the, 11, 33, 64
Franco, General, 22
French, Percy, 4
Freud, Sigmund, 80
Froude, James Anthony, 68

Gardiner family, 53
Gardiner Street, 32, 37
Gate Theatre, 54
General Post Office, 9, 37
Georgian Society, 56
Geraldine family of Kildare;
 see Leinster, Dukes of
Gladstone, William Ewart, 4
Gogarty, Oliver St John, 17, 19,
 39, 76
Goldsmith, Oliver, 22, 49–50
Good, James, 19
Gorman, Eric, 14
Grafton Street, 6, 54, 62, 69, 70
Grattan, Henry, 35, 53, 58, 59
Greene, David, 43
Gregory, Lady, 5, 13, 14–15
Griffith, Arthur, 39
Guinness's brewery, 58

Haddington Church, 83
Hall, F.G., 53
Ha'penny Bridge, the, 33
Harbottle, Mr Justice, 78–9
Harcourt Street, 3, 37
Healy, Tim, 80
Hell Fire Club, 55
Henrietta Street, 54
Howth, 25, 39, 89
Hyde, Douglas, 12–13

James, Henry, 78
John, Augustus, 76
Johnston, Francis, 37
Joyce, James, 9, 39, 80–83, 91

Kavanagh, Patrick, 13, 32, 35
Kenmare, Lord, 60
Kildare, Earl of, 54
Kildare, Marquess of, 70
Kildare Street Club, 66
Kilkenny, 51
Killiney, 23, 74
Kilmainham, 11, 47, 51
Kilmainham Prison, 11, 79, 85–8
King's Inns, 51, 83
Kingsbridge Station, 33

Larkin, Jim, 4
Lavin, Mary, 13, 22
Le Cleri (architect), 53
Le Fanu, Joseph, 78
Leeson Street, 37
Leinster, Dukes of, 44
Leinster House, 35, 51, 53, 54
Linenhall Barracks, 9–10
London, 45
Lugnaquilla, 24
Lynchehauen, James, 19

McCabe, Alexander, 5
McGahern, John, 14
Macpherson, James, 52
Mahaffy, Sir John, 19, 76–7
Mall, the, 54
Mallaghcleevaun, 24
Mangan, James Clarence, 68
Mansion House, 54
Markievicz, Constance, Countess, 9
Marx, Karl, 80
Maxwell, Constantia, 46

Mayhew, Henry, 69
Medmenham Abbey, 55
Merrion Square, 17, 28, 77
Molière, 15
Molyneux, brothers, 51, 54
Mooney, Ria, 14
Moore, George, 13, 24, 73
Moore, Tom, 35, 61, 68–9
Mountjoy Prison, 11
Mountjoy Square, 38

Napoleon, 63
National Library, 46
Nelson, Admiral Lord, 35, 36
Norbury, Lord, 65
North Circular Road, 15
Northern Ireland, 8, 27

O'Brien, Conor Cruise, 21
O'Brien, Flann, 13, 14
O'Brien, George, 53
O'Brien, William Smith, 71
O'Casey, Sean, 10, 14, 15–16
O'Connell, Daniel, 34, 35–6, 72
O'Connell Bridge, 5, 28
O'Connell Street, 5, 9, 32, 36, 37
O'Connor, Frank, 5, 13, 16
O'Connor, Sir James, 72
O'Faolain, Sean, 7, 13, 16, 42, 57
O'Flaherty, Liam, 13
O'Grady, Standish, 12
O'Higgins, Kevin, 6, 12
O'Neill, Eugene, 15
Ormonde, James, First Duke of,
  46–8

Ormonde, Dukes of, 44, 47
O'Trigger, Sir Lucius, 47

Palladio, Andrea, 53
Parliament House, 53
Parnell, Charles Stewart,
  35, 67, 79, 80, 86
Parnell Square, 67–8
Pearce, Edward, 53
Pearse, Patrick Henry,
  7, 8, 9, 10, 33, 80, 86
Perrault, Claude, 53
Phoenix Park, 36, 47, 55, 62, 79
Portobello, 9, 32
Powerscourt House, 51
Proust, Marcel, 80
Provost's House, 51
Pugin, Augustus Welby, 79

Rathmines, 66
Reid, Forrest, 49
Richards, Shelah, 14
Robinson, Lennox, 13, 14
Roche, Sir Boyle, 60, 62
Roche, Jem, 19–20
Roche, Tiger, 56, 75
Ross, Martin, 4, 75
Rosse, First Earl of, 55
Rotunda, the, 51, 54, 56
Royal Barracks, 70
Royal Dublin Society, 33, 49, 73
Royal Hospital, Kilmainham, 47, 51
Ruskin, John, 52
Russell, George William; *see* AE
Rutland Square, 33

St Andrew's Church, 66
St Catherine's Church, 65
St George's Church, 67
St Mary's Chapel of Ease
   (the Black Church), 66–7, 83
St Patrick's Cathedral, 38, 44, 47
St Stephen's Green,
   5, 9, 17, 35, 37, 54, 56, 57, 79
Sandycove, 39
Scott, Michael, 14
Scott, Sir Walter, 69
Sea Point, 38, 39
Serlio, Sebastiano, 53
Shaw, George Bernard, 13, 17-18, 26, 74
Sheilds, Arthur, 14
Shelbourne Hotel, 73, 79
Sheridan, Richard Brinsley, 68, 74
Skeffington, Francis, 9
Somerville, Edith, 4, 75
Soper (Reform Club chef), 70
Stephen's Green;
   see St Stephen's Green
Stephens, James, 5, 13
Strindberg, Johan August, 15
Strong, L. A. G., 15, 39–40
Sugar Loaf Mountains, 23
Swift, Jonathan, 49, 50–51, 52, 79
Synge, John Millington, 5, 13, 76

Temper, John, 66
Thackeray, William Makepeace, 30, 73
Thomas Street, 65
Tone, Wolfe, 9, 34, 53, 54, 59, 60, 62–4
Trinity College, 35, 45, 52–3, 66
Trinity College Library, 45, 49, 51, 52

Trollope, Anthony, 30

University Club, 35
University of Dublin;
   see Dublin University
Upper Castle Yard, 51
Upper Rutland Street, 67
Ussher, Aarland, 4, 25, 89

Valera, Eamon de, 9, 19–20
Vanbrugh, Sir John, 53
Viceregal Lodge, 33, 37
Victoria, Queen, 35, 70–71
Vignola, Giacoma, 53
Viola, G., 53

Waterloo Road, 6
Wellington Road, 66
Wesley, John, 59
West, Robert, 56
Westland Row Station, 3, 84
Westmoreland Street, 32
Whaley, Buck, 56, 75
White, Terence de Vere, 8, 12
Wicklow Hills, 24
Wilde, Oscar, 74, 77
Wilde, Dr (later Sir) William, 77–8
Wilde, Mrs William (later Lady), 77
William of Orange, 34, 35, 48
Wine-Tavern Street, 47
Woodham Smith, Cecil, 69, 70
Woodward, Benjamin, 79

Yeats, W. B., 5, 13, 16–18, 68, 80
Yeats, Mrs W. B., 17